T0306040

"Your book is a masterpiece. I feel I have been the guest of honour at a glorious feast: of knowledge and understanding; of interweaving and parsing; of outrageous complexity and internal, dependable, grand and glorious simplicity; and of love and deep regard for the original master-piece that is the human being. You have done humanity justice. I thank you for your book's richness, its challenge, its kindness, its depth, its care and coherence in our careless and chaotic world. Please know most of all that your book is a treasure, one I am honoured to have read and to have forever."

Nancy Kline, author of *Time to Think:*
Listening to ignite the human mind (1999),
developer of the Thinking Environment®,
and founder of Time to Think Inc.

"*Dancing Through the Storm* is an authoritative new approach to leader-ship. It addresses how leaders can succeed in business through build-ing relationships and creating a culture of psychological safety in a very competitive world. The author's approach is underpinned by Ken Wilber's Integral model and Nancy Kline's Thinking Environment, greatly enhanced by the considerable expertise and experience she brings to leadership, diversity and inclusion from her practice. This work truly presents, as the title promises, 'an Integral approach to transformative leadership'. Dorrian advances the compelling case that leaders need to be coaches rather than constantly in command and control. Innovative and practical, her stories, case studies and examples, while from South Africa, highlight the need for global leaders to address the challenges of complexity, diversity and culture at every turn. With Wilber's model as the framework, she guides leaders through their most difficult task: not just running a business, but leading people. Her insights into Nancy Kline's Thinking Environment underlines not only the vital role of building relationships, if leaders are to be successful, but the ability to foster a listening culture. The book delves deeply into resolving conflict, as well as examining leader identity construction, the brain's addiction to prediction, and the critical importance of building trust in an organi-sation. A thoroughly stimulating and original contribution to leadership studies."

Sunny Stout-Rostron, Stellenbosch Business School,
University of Stellenbosch, Cape Town, South Africa;
Founding President of Coaches and
Mentors of South Africa (COMENSA).

"Ken Wilber, developer of the Integral theoretical framework for growth and development, is the author of over 20 books. Yet anybody look-ing for an integrated developmental methodology in Wilber's work will not find one – his view is 'work it out for yourself'. As a result, many practitioners have had to develop tools to make it practically possible for individuals to use Wilber's Integral theory to improve their lives. Dorrian has worked hard at this; in this book she shows via case studies how to use the Integral AQAL model within a coaching context, what types of question can be used to cover all four quadrants, how that enables the client to make sense of their own experience, and how to work with Wilber's different lines of development. Staying true to Wilber's message that any theory is not 'the truth' but 'a truth', including his own, Dorrian then shows in a very practical way how Nancy Kline's Thinking Environment and the Enneagram can easily be integrated into Wilber's model. As a result, coaches interested in Wilber's work will find this book a very welcome addition to their library. It is written in a very clear, logical, and practical way. I admire her ability to take a complex theory and make it very simple and practical."

Lloyd Chapman, author of *Integrated Experiential Coaching: Becoming an executive coach* (2010) and *The Evidence-Based Practitioner Coach: Understanding the Integrated Experiential Learning Process* (2023).

"It has been my privilege to know Dorrian as a friend and colleague for two decades. Most importantly, she is one of the most ethical, honest and direct people I have ever known; I am very envious of her students. Despite her academic background (two Doctorates), she is a very pragmatic practitioner who uses her knowledge to teach and to coach in an everyday sort of way. This book is a distillation of her knowledge and utilisation of the Integral model, and makes a valuable contribution to the fields of coaching and leadership. In it, readers will find relevant case studies that bring the models to life in ways the reader will be able to use immediately in their own contexts."

Peter McNab, author of *Towards an Integral Vision: Using NLP and Ken Wilber's AQAL model to enhance communication* (2005).

"The challenges facing leaders have arguably never been greater than they are today. And transformative leadership – the kind of leadership that transforms individuals, teams and societies – is essential to navigating these challenges. But how do we – as leaders, psychologists, human resources practitioners and coaches – develop the approaches and skills to support and become transformative leaders? Dorrian Aiken's book is a timely and inspiring answer to this question, in which she shares her deep insights into leadership and organisational behaviour. Many business books stop there, which leaves the reader feeling half-inspired and half-intimidated, and wondering how on earth to apply the lessons in real life. The beauty of this work is that Aiken also offers clear, evidence-based theories that give us a practical framework for interpreting her insights and applying them to our own situations. She draws on influential approaches like the Thinking Environment, psychological safety and Integral coaching, applies them to actual cases, and pulls it all together in this step-by-step guide to developing transformative leadership capacity. While all leaders and coaches will benefit from it, I think the book will strike a special chord with the leaders of diverse teams. Want practical tips on how to build employee engagement or run more inclusive meetings? Read this book! Want to become a better coach or a better leader? Read this book!"

Shelagh Goodwin, Industrial and Organisation Psychologist;
GM: Human Resources, Media24.

"This book equips coaches to embed their practice in the organisations and other complex systems in which their clients operate. This is one of the most accessible distillations of Integral coaching and the Thinking Environment which I have read. The book provides an excellent synthesis of cutting-edge theories, and is essential reading for coaches seeking to work systemically. Fascinating case studies are woven throughout the book, with reflective commentary that gives immediate insight into guidelines for practice. This book has the potential to substantially evolve the practice of coaching."

Roger Maitland, Director: LifeLab;
adjunct faculty member, Stellenbosch Business School,
University of Stellenbosch, Cape Town.

"This book is as much a gift to the coach as to those being coached. Dorrian started working with us when we were beginning a company restructure, with a vision of creating a more empowered organisation and giving leaders more autonomy. Her style of starting with the leadership group and coaching them using the Integral quadrants proved invaluable. I have seen the power of this method on the leadership team and the company as a whole. I see huge growth in individual leaders who I now lean on for advice and perspective. While seemingly complicated, I never appreciated the full method until reading the book, as it was handled with understanding of what we needed at each stage, and at a pace where we could implement change rather than just understanding theory. It is quite amusing to reflect on the process this far, and see how a strong coach gently nudges you through the complexity of change. As I learn more, I see clarity in the direction and methods used which helps me manage the change still required. Enjoy the journey."

Diane Wilson, Joint CEO, VMLY&R South Africa.

"In my experience running several businesses I have seen a pattern of conflict emerge between those leaders committed to the old 'command and control' model and the younger generation who actively resist attempts to override their freedom and agency. This represents a challenge to managers that demands an entirely new skillset. Dorrian Aiken has provided a thorough and thoughtful blueprint for how modern leaders can not only face this challenge, but turn it to their advantage. Standing on the shoulders of thinkers like Wilber and Kline, she has pulled together an entire operating system for how to build thriving, happy, and fulfilling workplaces. Step-by-step, she walks the reader through an Integrally-informed approach, explaining in clear and straightforward terms why the methods make sense and how to apply them. In the work Dorrian has done with our own organisation I have seen tangible changes in how people work together and how their leadership maturity has evolved. This book makes it possible for leaders everywhere to absorb this approach and start manifesting real change to their culture and employee satisfaction. If you have yearned to see people loving their work, learning, growing and collaborating, this book is the first step toward opening up new potential in your business. We will be using these tools again and again in the future of our business. If you read one book on leadership this year make it this one. You – and your team – will not emerge from it without visible improvement."

Jarred Cinman, Joint CEO, VMLY&R South Africa.

"With this book, the author graciously shares her profound knowledge and experience as coach, specialising in Integral theory and the creation of a Thinking Environment. By sharing her wealth of experience in coaching through the lenses of an experiential learner and master-reflector, she takes the reader on a journey of possibility, reminding us how key relationships are to navigate complex situations with resilience. To my mind, how to cultivate inclusivity is the single most important quest of our time. The work-based focus is meaningful for both professional coaches and leaders of organisations and teams. It might not rain today, but I feel like a tango after reading this book. Thanks, Dr Dorrian Aiken!"

Salome van Coller-Peter, Associate Professor:
Leadership Coaching, Stellenbosch Business School,
University of Stellenbosch.

An Integral Approach to Transformative Leadership

Dancing Through the Storm

This essential new book is a practical "how-to" guide to enhancing the quality of relationships between leaders and individuals in organisations – the proven key to maximising performance, building resilience, and retaining talent.

Integral vision, seen through each of the four quadrants described in this book, gives access to a range of perspectives, irreducible to one another but each significant in adding a kaleidoscope of understanding to a topic or body of knowledge. The author draws on recent research which focuses on Integral theory and emphasises the benefits to an organisation, including cultivating, at several levels, leaders and teams through coaching, improving the quality of meetings, introducing an understanding of emotional intelligence, and more recently, addressing adult stages of development. The book also demonstrates how the Integral quadrants can bring clarity to interpersonal and cross-sector communication, especially in diagnosing, planning, and implementing team and organisational strategy.

The concepts and practical skills explored in this book will be a valuable resource for senior leaders, human resources specialists, and in-house and external coaches focusing on leadership development, as well as students and trainers of coaching.

Dorrian Aiken PhD DProf is an Integral Master Coach™, a certified Thinking Environment® coach and consultant, and a founding member of the Time to Think® Collegiate in South Africa. She lectures in leadership coaching at the University of Stellenbosch. Her passion is developing leaders at every level to implement a culture of inclusivity in organisations.

The Professional Coaching Series

This series brings together leading exponents and researchers in the coaching field to provide a definitive set of core texts important to the development of the profession. It aims to meet two needs – a professional series that provides the core texts that are theoretically and experimentally grounded, and a practice series covering forms of coaching based in evidence. Together they provide a complementary framework to introduce, promote and enhance the development of the coaching profession.

Titles in the series:

Coaching on the Axis
Working with Complexity in Business and Executive Coaching
By Marc Simon Kahn

Business Coaching International
Transforming Individuals and Organizations, 2nd Edition
By Sunny Stout-Rostron

Swings and Roundabouts
A Self-Coaching Workbook for Parents and Those Considering Becoming Parents
By Agnes Bamford

Internal Coaching
The Inside Story
By Katharine St John-Brooks

Coaching in Education
Getting Better Results for Students, Educators, and Parents
By Christian van Nieuwerburgh

Coaching in the Family Owned Business
A Path to Growth
By David A. Lane

Integrated Experiential Coaching
Becoming an Executive Coach
By Lloyd Chapman

The Art of Inspired Living
Coach Yourself with Positive Psychology
By Sarah Corrie

For further information about this series please visit https://www.routledge.com/The-Professional-Coaching-Series/book-series/KARNPROFC

An Integral Approach to Transformative Leadership

Dancing Through the Storm

Dorrian Aiken

Routledge
Taylor & Francis Group
LONDON AND NEW YORK

Designed cover image: © Getty Images

First published 2024
by Routledge
4 Park Square, Milton Park, Abingdon, Oxon OX14 4RN

and by Routledge
605 Third Avenue, New York, NY 10158

Routledge is an imprint of the Taylor & Francis Group, an informa business

© 2024 Dorrian Aiken

British Library Cataloguing-in-Publication Data
A catalogue record for this book is available from the British Library

Library of Congress Cataloging-in-Publication Data
Names: Aiken, Dorrian Elizabeth, author.
Title: An integral approach to transformative leadership: dancing through the storm / Dorrian Elizabeth Aiken.
Description: Abingdon, Oxon ; New York, NY : Routledge, 2024. | Series: The professional coaching series | Includes bibliographical references and index. | Summary: "This essential new book is a practical "how-to" guide to enhancing the quality of relationships between leaders and individuals in organisations - the proven key to maximising performance, building resilience, and retaining talent. Integral Vision, seen through each of the four quadrants described in this book, gives access to a range of perspectives, irreducible to one another but each significant in adding a kaleidoscope of understanding to a topic or body of knowledge. The author draws on recent research which focuses on Integral theory and emphasises the benefits to an organisation, including cultivating, at several levels, leaders and teams through coaching, improving the quality of meetings, introducing an understanding of emotional intelligence, and more recently, addressing adult stages of development. The book also demonstrates how the Integral quadrants can bring clarity to interpersonal and cross-sector communication, especially in diagnosing, planning and implementing team and organisational strategy. The concepts and practical skills explored in this book will be a valuable resource for senior leaders, human resources specialists, in-house and external coaches focussing on leadership development, as well as students and trainers of coaching"- Provided by publisher.
Identifiers: LCCN 2023016116 (print) | LCCN 2023016117 (ebook) | ISBN 9781032454856 (hardback) | ISBN 9781032454832 (paperback) | ISBN 9781003377221 (ebook)
Subjects: LCSH: Leadership.
Classification: LCC HD57.7 .A39 2024 (print) | LCC HD57.7 (ebook) | DDC 658.4/092–dc23/eng/20230428
LC record available at https://lccn.loc.gov/2023016116
LC ebook record available at https://lccn.loc.gov/2023016117

ISBN: 978-1-032-45485-6 (hbk)
ISBN: 978-1-032-45483-2 (pbk)
ISBN: 978-1-003-37722-1 (ebk)

DOI: 10.4324/9781003377221

Typeset in Times New Roman
by Deanta Global Publishing Services, Chennai, India

Contents

Illustrations

About the author

Dr Aiken holds a PhD (University of Exeter) and a Doctorate in Professional Studies (University of Middlesex). She is an Integral Master Coach™, a certified Thinking Environment® coach and consultant, and a founding member of the Time to Think® Collegiate in South Africa. She has studied Integral leadership at the Integral Institute and attended the Leadership Maturity Framework and Development Intensive for Professionals with Susanne Cook-Greuter. Her passion is developing leaders at every level to implement a culture of inclusivity in organisations. She focuses on developing their ability to use coaching competencies as a core part of their leadership style. She also is experienced in working with cultural diversity issues and inclusivity in the workplace.

She is an adjunct faculty member lecturing in leadership coaching at the Business School of the University of Stellenbosch, and a facilitator of executive leadership development programmes at the Graduate School of Business of the University of Cape Town.

Her research areas include applications of Integral theory, in particular stages of adult development, and the implications of neuroscience for relationship management in organisations.

Foreword

The time has come for this book. I have been aware of Dorrian's work for many years. She has consistently been interested in diversity, complexity, and ways to help leaders integrate listening cultures, psychological safety, and ways of being fully present. Bringing together the work of Ken Wilber and Nancy Kline, other key authors, and her own extensive research and practice, she seeks to enhance the quality of relationships between individuals and organisations. It is a delight to finally see the strands of her work represented in this latest addition to our Professional Coaching Series.

Her ideas will, I am sure, be of interest to both coaches and leaders adopting a coaching style in their work. Using an integration of theoretical perspectives, case studies, and practice examples, she elaborates frameworks for enhancing performance, building resilience, and retaining talent.

The central tenet of her work is that the quality of relationships is key. She does not offer this as a generic formula for successful coaching and leadership, however, but rather seeks to identify key relationship aspects that impact in different ways across different contexts. This provides a detailed, informed, and intelligent approach to generating individual and organisational change.

Two features are particularly important. Firstly, Dorrian's approach draws on Integral concepts (from Ken Wilber) that cover areas such as ways of knowing, seeing, and doing, and focus in particular on connectedness between individuals and networks. Secondly, her approach is linked to the use of a Thinking Environment® (from Nancy Kline) which creates the context for interaction based on mutual regard. Hence, ways of thinking about people in their world are linked to processes to explore change.

These concepts are placed within the current issues facing corporate life, where complexity and messy or wicked problems generate frustration with traditional approaches. Dorrian uses examples from work on reinventing organisations, agile transformations, and meta-frameworks for organisational challenges to explore the fast-changing and unpredictable world we face. She urges us to reimagine existing systems and structures to ensure more satisfaction, at several levels from the personal to the professional.

Her metaphor of "dancing through the storm" points to the coach and leader being able to know the dance steps and how to execute them – which, of course, also means knowing the dance partner well. She leads the reader through the need for such partners to be self-aware, to engage with different worldviews, to keep their balance (and the necessary quality of attention) when buffeted by crosswinds, and to ensure they are able to either move with the current or resist it, as needed.

These concepts underpin the chapters that follow where cases, examples, concepts, and tools are brought into play to enable leaders and coaches to engage in continuous practice on the job. In this way, coaching and leadership are not separate, but integral to the work.

Each chapter explores a key element of the journey through which she takes the reader. Integral theory is examined through a case study which enhances understanding of the frameworks to prepare for the dance steps to follow. The way this frame can enable awareness of our sweet spots and blind spots is used to explore the window on the world that influences our perceptions and hence practices. The use of these different windows (or quadrants in Wilber's terms) is demonstrated through another case enabling a senior manager to improve both management style and team co-operation. A really interesting issue relates to how people at loggerheads can learn that it is not about who is right and wrong but that they are seeing the world through different perspectives, and how such conflicts can become mirrored across an organisation. This is explored further through an examination of the impact of discrimination on the climate of an organisation. A further chapter builds upon our understanding of the way a listening culture can transform an organisation by reframing assumptions to release the energy to improve outcomes. The role of the Enneagram (which I have also found useful for work in family businesses) is given additional value through its use to explore sweet spots and blind spots. Stages of human development are introduced to further enhance the ways we can help people to build their capacity. The tendency to hold "either/or" perspectives which so dismantle productive thinking is replaced with a "both/and" approach. The final chapter draws together the themes throughout to illustrate practical ways to work with the concepts to enhance both coaching and leadership.

It is the thoughtful and careful use of case material throughout the book that brings to life the theoretical concepts to build an intelligent and useful framework for the reader. For all those who have followed our Professional Coaching Series (and our thanks to you), we commend this insightful new addition. It will intrigue, inform, challenge, often delight, and always offer valuable tools to enhance practice for both coaches and leaders.

Professor David A. Lane
Professional Development Foundation
Series Editor: Professional Coaching Series

Preface

My main purpose in writing this book has been to share with student coaches and business clients the concepts and practices that have been the focus of my doctoral research and professional work for the past 20 years – namely, Integral vision and its impact on leadership. For students of coaching, my objective is to simplify access to this ever-increasing field of research. I also share the models and tools I have used in working with leaders at various levels in organisations. I am fortunate in having amassed over the years substantial evidence on what has been positively impactful.

"There is nothing as practical as a good theory", stated the pioneering applied psychologist Kurt Lewin (1943: 118, quoted in Endrejat and Burnes, 2022: 3), at a time when psychology as a field was rich in theory but often lacking in practical ways to test and apply theory to real-world problems. In contrast, Ken Wilber's Integral vision (theory) has been successfully applied in practice over the past two decades to several disciplines, including psychology, medicine, architecture, art, education, environmental sustainability, and increasingly in recent years to business and change management. Each area of study has benefited from Integral vision's comprehensive and inclusive approach. Integral vision is a meta-theory – it gives access through its lenses to a range of perspectives, irreducible to one another but each significant in adding a kaleidoscope of understanding to a topic or body of knowledge. As Wilber points out in each of his many books, Integral theory needs some explanation before it can be applied. I have offered a summary in the book of core principles of the Integral approach, emphasising practical application, and keeping it simple (hopefully not reductionist), in the expectation that what I have tried out is repeatable and helpful for others.

Many articles and books cited in the book and listed in the Bibliography focus on Integral theory in meeting the challenges of transformative leadership. They emphasise the benefits to an organisation of cultivating, at several levels, the leaders and teams through coaching, improving the quality of meetings, introducing an understanding of emotional intelligence, and more recently, addressing adult stages of development. In the increasingly complex and rapidly changing world of work, an Integral perspective usefully connects these multiple layers, which are often treated separately to the detriment of organisational life.

Dorrian Aiken

Acknowledgements

I am grateful for the encouragement of colleagues at the University of Stellenbosch Business School, and thankful to the Integral Institute in Boulder, Colorado, and Integral Coaching Canada Inc. for the most complete experiential learning in translating theory into practice. Words of gratitude do not do justice to the impact of Nancy Kline's training and writings on the course of my personal and professional life. Thank you to Lloyd Chapman, who introduced me to Ken Wilber's work; to very dear Integral life-partners Anna Cowen and John Ziniades, for always being there; to special friend, Peter McNab, for illustrating the Enneagram on a sandy beach; to fellow coach Jeremy Clampett, for his keen eye and encouragement; and to my husband, Geoff Blake, who has grounded me with his steadfast support.

Dedicated to the late Margaret Legum, dear friend, whose humanity and far-sighted vision for a fairer world changed lives for the better.

Dorrian Aiken

Introduction

About this book

During Hurricane Ida, a devastating hurricane that lashed the state of Louisiana in 2021, I watched in awe as a CNN reporter struggled to stay on his feet with his microphone and to communicate clearly while being buffeted on a sea wall by gale-force winds. His efforts reminded me of the challenge leaders have in staying on their feet, projecting calm in the midst of a storm – it takes courage, focus, and fitness. For a good coach and leader, fitness means so much more than the physical – it requires first and foremost self-awareness, the capacity to reflect, to balance multiple perspectives, to manage complexity with resilience, and to sponsor innovation.

Not too long ago, two prominent exponents of coaching, Michael Cavanagh and David Lane (2012), saw the need for coaches to increase their capacity to deal with complex non-linear systems, building relationships and resilience within individuals and organisations. This observation appealed to me because I have found myself over time engaged less with coaching individuals in private one-on-one sessions, and more drawn to finding ways to work with leaders at any level, on the job, in relation to their colleagues, teams, and stakeholders. The demands on the coach shift exponentially in helping leaders manage complex systems. In the words of Pamela McLean from her book packed with resources, *Self as Coach, Self as Leader*:

> Those of us coaching senior leaders need to understand organisational systems, the field of leadership, the challenges of today's world of work, and the volatile world in which we live. The old belief that a good coach can coach anyone no longer holds up.
>
> (McLean, 2019: xxi)

A particular viewpoint has informed my entire working life: every output, good and bad, depends on *the quality of the relationship* between individuals, within families, within teams and organisations, and across cultures. This book is an account of my practical experiences of the past 20 years, informed by this outlook, of a

DOI: 10.4324/9781003377221-1

particular approach to coaching leaders. There are two core influences embodied in my framework: Ken Wilber's Integral vision and his Integral Operating System, and Nancy Kline's principles and practices in creating a Thinking Environment®. Their use is further enhanced by models and tools selected for their potential to enlarge the experience of organisations and teams in building a culture of adaptability and emotional resilience.

The Integral Operating System has five elements: quadrants, lines (of intelligence), stages or levels of development, states (of awareness), and types. Together, these elements map the relationship among multiple layers in knowing, seeing, and doing. Much of the focus in this book is on making use of the foundational element of the *quadrants*: these four perspectives integrate and connect what should be evident to most of us – that each of us is an *individual*, with thoughts and feelings, skills and behaviours, and at the same time, we are also *connected* to others in many ways – family, friends, work, sport, religion, and culture. For better or worse, these groups are connected to larger entities – social networks, organisations, culture, systems, and nations. Connections have consequences. Especially significant in the Integral Operating System is the emphasis on *stages of personal and collective development*: individuals have the potential to develop through stages of increasing complexity over the course of their lives, along several dimensions of intelligence. Social systems, teams, and organisations are similarly capable of stages of development, of transformative growth. This book's case studies offer individual and organisational change examples, mapped on the quadrant domains of individual subjectivity, individual behaviours, collective values or culture, and systems, as discussed in Chapter 1.

In my experience, introducing the conditions for a Thinking Environment early in working with leaders and their teams enables an atmosphere of positive engagement and mutual regard, despite interpersonal challenges and conflicts. The practice of meeting this way tends to raise the emotional intelligence of groups, in addition to that of individuals, as a consequence of its rules of engagement. The consistently positive feedback from groups who experience this way of engaging one-on-one and in meetings confirms Nancy Kline's words, "We should create a Thinking Environment because it works. Because everything depends on it. And because if you get good at it, you have a tool for life" (Kline, 1999: 21).

Frustration in the world of work

There is a sentiment currently that Integral theory's time has come as a way of seeing and interpreting complexity, a view for which there is ample evidence in the books and articles that are surfacing on frustrations with traditional corporate life. It has been suggested, for example, that 2020 was

> the year when all of the right conditions and contradictions for Integral finally emerged – a cascade of "wicked problems" that can only be fully seen,

let alone solved, from an Integral point of view, but whose effects can be felt by virtually *everybody*.

(DeVos, 2020: 1)

Frédéric Laloux's (2014) influential work *Reinventing Organisations: A Guide to Creating Organisations Inspired by the Next Stage of Human Consciousness*, with a comprehensive introduction by Ken Wilber, gives examples of organisations guided by Integral vision, with advice on the steps to better organisational life. More recently, Michael Spayd and Michelle Madore (an Integral coach), demonstrate a thorough application of Ken Wilber's Integral Operating System as a meta-framework for organisational systemic change in *Agile Transformation: Using the Integral Agile Transformation Framework® to Think and Lead Differently* (Spayd and Madore, 2021). Landrum and Gardner (2012) maintain that Integral theory, as an encompassing meta-theory, should be the new lens through which comprehensive definitions of organisational roles and responsibilities are interpreted.

Two themes in all these works predominate: the demands of the twenty-first century and our fast-changing, unpredictable VUCA world (an acronym adopted by the business world from the US military describing volatile, unpredictable, complex, and ambiguous conditions), and frustration with the world of work that is organised in ways that no longer satisfy. And indeed, increasingly, I meet with clients who want to transform their current way of operating to something that works and feels "much better". "Much better" is as vague as it sounds – but it inevitably includes the wish to re-imagine existing systems, structures, and roles to ensure more personal and professional satisfaction for themselves.

Leaders as transformative coaches

A good part of their satisfaction would result from a thriving business with employees who are energised, engaged, and happy to come to work. Just how much complexity, resilience, focus, and dedication that wish entails, in order to embark on this dance of transformation, a dance in an unpredictable storm of change, depends on the degree of self-work a leader practises. Whether we are challenged by change at the macro level of our global environment or at the micro level of our immediate context, the dance of transformation calls on an interlocking set of skills and practices that are as yet fragile and emergent in human behaviour, as Clare Graves (1974) suggested in his prescient article "Human Nature Prepares for a Momentous Leap".

Themes running through the book

To carry further the metaphor in the sub-title, *Dancing Through the Storm*, coach and leader need to know the key steps of this dance, how to sequence them and execute them superbly – and know how to partner well:

- Both coach and leader need to be *self-aware*, and to have committed to consistent practice – the fabled 10,000 hours of self-observation practice.
- It means knowing how to understand and engage with different and competing *worldviews*.
- The art of keeping the beat and your balance in the teeth of violent crosswinds is the harmony of the steps you practise on *certain key lines of intelligence* – core leadership competencies to which all normally functioning adults have access.
- Your perfect balance and that of others around you depends on the focus and *quality of the attention* you pay. The commitment to *listening* and its rules of engagement are essential to establish at leadership level.
- The evidence found in *neuroscience* gives incentive to coaches and leaders for focusing on better ways of relating: the way we are treated has an impact on our brains, our wellness, and our capacity to think clearly.
- Both coaches and leaders benefit from listening carefully to the drift of the currents in social spaces, how quickly people are swept along by the dominant current (culture), internalising the *rules of the game*, for better or worse. Who has positional power, who is rewarded, who is overlooked?

Coaching with an Integral lens

Leadership at its best is a form of coaching, dare I say. The leader-as-coach is transformational more than transactional: leading by example, intending to inspire and motivate, and encouraging brave thinking by sharing strengths and weaknesses (Bass and Avolio, 1994.) These are the functions of a good coach *and* the characteristics of good leadership. Ibarra and Scoular (2019) confirm the increasing trend for companies to invest in training leaders and managers at all levels as coaches in order to adapt to constantly changing environments. So, a core focus of my Integral approach is to support those leaders who want to be transformational by embracing a coaching style.

Research by Lisa Frost (2009) reviewed prominent coaching models through an Integral lens, revealing the majority of them to be partial in their emphasis of a particular view of reality. She shares the view of Joanne Hunt of Integral Coaching Canada Inc. that most coaching schools or models tend to adopt a particular perspective as the focus of a client's coaching journey, with a loss of engagement with other perspectives present in the client's objectives (Hunt, 2009).

An Integral view of many of the well-known coaching models, like John Whitmore's GROW (Whitmore, 2009), David Rock's ARIA (Rock, 2009), and Peter Hawkins' CLEAR (Hawkins and Smith, 2013), would conjecture that they are more accurately an orienting scaffold or framework – structures that hold key compass points in the coaching journey. A guide to structure, no matter how useful, is not an entire picture of a complex system. To use the metaphor of a house, it is much more than its structure. Its interior and décor tell an idiosyncratic story that includes the efficiency of the overall design, and the operational effectiveness of its systems like plumbing and electricity supply. The choice of functional items like which coffee machine or vacuum cleaner is in use gives an array of data which could suggest the purchasing power available to the inhabitants, as well as raising more subjective conjecture on aesthetic awareness. More than a structure, the Integral Operating System makes sure that every element and angle of the client's reality is explored – subjective experience, worldview, objective contexts, actions, behaviours, and dimensions of relationship. The multiple perspectives offered by Integral vision help coach and leader firstly to explore and map the current territory as accurately as possible (diagnosis), and secondly, to plot and calibrate adjustments, and then put new processes into practice to reach the desired outcomes in each dimension of their system (planning and evaluation).

Each chapter illustrates a practical aspect of working with an Integral approach, in particular to demonstrate the versatility of the foundational element of the Integral Operating System – the quadrants. Client stories give examples of behaviours and incidents, of actions that were taken, and tools that were brought into play. The aim of this approach to transformative coaching is to support leaders in *continuous practice on the job*.

The chapters

Chapter 1: Mastering the dance: First steps

Wilber's theory of Integral vision is explained in brief: his Integral Operating System and its foundational element, the quadrants. A client site is introduced, where the CEO and his Executive Committee (ExCo) express the desire to transform the company culture from a climate of distrust and poor performance to one of positive engagement. An aspect of the quadrants' flexibility is demonstrated in this chapter by illustrating their use as a *diagnostic tool* to surface unexpressed opinions in order to plan a culture transformation project.

Chapter 2: Sweet spots and blind spots

The next step in initiating the transformation project is to coach members of the ExCo using the Integral quadrants, building on the mapping and planning from the first meeting described in Chapter 1. A crucial understanding for one ExCo member is his recognition of a preferred quadrant as his window on the world – his "sweet spot"; and he also becomes aware of his neglected areas of perception – his "blind spots".

Chapter 3: A four-quadrant coaching conversation

Coaching with the quadrants leads a senior manager to become aware of behaviours that need to change in order to improve team co-operation and earn more positive feedback on her management style – a promotion rests on the outcome.

Chapter 4: True – but partial: "I am right, and I can prove it"

Two people at loggerheads, both with evidence that the other is to blame, discover with the help of the quadrants that while each of their versions is truthful, they are partial. Willingness on both sides to see the missing pieces reframes a hostile relationship to one of accommodation. Their conflicting points of view are mirrored in six recurring narratives circulating in the organisation which inflame conflict.

Chapter 5: Leading the dance of inclusivity

Key members of the management come together to explore the "me, we, world" of bias and the impact of discrimination on the climate of an organisation – using the quadrants with teams to reframe shared values and align with shared purpose.

Chapter 6: Leading a listening culture

From senior leaders to the shopfloor, initiating a listening culture has the effect of raising the emotional intelligence of all employees. In the first place, it transforms what might be a harmful knee-jerk response into a considered reflection; secondly, its ability to raise and reframe untrue and inhibiting limiting assumptions releases positive energy, with the potential to improve performance outcomes. This chapter focuses on the work of Nancy Kline (1999, 2009, 2020) in managing meetings.

Chapter 7: The Enneagram: Self-awareness and relationship management

Follow the journey of a company's use of the Enneagram combined with the Integral quadrants as a way of introducing individuals and teams to their motivations, values, thinking styles, and ways of solving problems. More than personality typing, the Enneagram expands individuals' insight into their quadrant sweet spots and blind spots (discussed in Chapter 2); and it creates multiple pathways for increasing team co-operation.

Chapter 8: Onwards and upwards: Leadership and stages of adult development

Each of the four quadrants shows stages or levels of human development, not as rigid steps, but as fluid, wave-like processes. A baby must crawl before walking; we learn progressively to master complex skills. Discover how an individual chooses practices to increase reflective awareness – small steps that shift them and the people they lead to building more capacity in dealing with complexity and ambiguity.

Chapter 9: Revisiting "both-and": Working with polarities

A case study reveals the wisdom of holding a "both-and" perspective rather than "either-or" mindset as a means of resolving conflict. Polarities, the concept of Barry Johnson (2014), resolve the impasse of problems for which there is no single solution; the approach describes a process of creating practical "both-and" outcomes. Johnson's approach dismantles conflict through its ability to include the views held by managers at most stages found in organisations, from the least complex to the most.

Chapter 10: In conclusion

This chapter draws together the themes in each of the preceding chapters and relates these to the needs of leadership in our current world. Each chapter has illustrated practical ways of working with the foundational element of Ken Wilber's Integral Operating System – the quadrants. The concept of leader-as-coach and the requisite skills is explored. The overarching message is *connection*: consciously bringing into awareness four always-present aspects of human reality, and working with that awareness to increase leadership potential for resilience in managing complexity, ambiguity, and uncertainty.

Chapter 1

Mastering the dance

First steps

The background

The Managing Director of Asset Management South Africa (AMSA) (not its real name), a relatively small financial services company of 80 staff, was puzzled: he believed he had the best Executive Committee he had worked with in quite a while, yet the staff surveys told a very different story. He needed to understand why the members of the leadership team were receiving such negative feedback, when he believed they were focusing on all the right things. The MD outlined his strategic focus as the drive to grow the business and regain the company's position among the top asset management companies on the Johannesburg Stock Exchange, despite a complex and rapidly changing environment in South Africa since its political transition from apartheid in 1994. To this end, and recognising the impact of poor staff morale on future success, he announced the roll-out of three concurrent projects to increase productivity through an enabling and transformed culture of inclusivity.

The negative feedback from internal climate and culture surveys highlighted that most neglected at AMSA were the *relationships* between the leaders and their employees. The MD believed the overall goal of these three projects depended on positive and sustainable change through the leadership in the way all teams and individuals behaved throughout the business. To that end, he committed himself and his Executive Committee (ExCo) to coaching, in the hope of better collaboration. Adam Kahane (2017) has a word of caution regarding what collaboration might mean: that the conventional assumption that everyone is on the same page and in agreement with what needs to be done, is wrong.

AMSA was the perfect organisation for working with leadership challenges. The rapid pace of transformation experienced by the company, driven by internal and external demands, compounded existing issues that surfaced in the employee surveys. There had been several previous attempts by the ExCo to address perceived problems. It appeared that these attempts resulted in the many different strands that created the current conditions being conflated: multiple causes of dysfunction were being addressed by single cause-and-effect solutions which ultimately failed to gain traction. The organisation had previously engaged with several consultants and change management processes, each working from strict methodological

DOI: 10.4324/9781003377221-2

principles. The impact of these had been a series of well-conceived but piecemeal interventions, the benefits of which unravelled under the weight of multiple ongoing issues. Having had an insight, through our coaching sessions, into Integral theory and its business application, the MD was keen to work with an approach that might bring people issues and business systems and practices into a united focus.

Integral vision – a brief introduction

Ken Wilber is probably the world's best-known exponent of Integral theory. He is, however, quick to acknowledge the several influential thinkers who have impacted his development – Jean Gebser, Abraham Maslow, Jürgen Habermas, Arthur Koestler, Sri Aurobindo, Clare Graves, Ernst Schumacher, and Jan Smuts, to name a few. Integral theory holds that we have access today to knowledge of all the world's cultures, their histories and developmental or evolutionary stages; we have access to multiple sources of knowledge on topics that traditionally have been studied individually – for example, science, art, sociology, psychology, history, anthropology, mathematics, politics, and economics. Integral vision sees that each topic in itself can have multiple facets – for instance, mathematics includes algebra, geometry, and trigonometry, all of which can be separate studies – and that topics or knowledge sources are interconnected. To examine a topic without reference to multiple sources, perspectives, and influences would be incomplete. As Wilber (2001c: 8) would put it, the study would be *true – but partial*.

Wilber designed a model, the Integral Operating System, in order to map this enormous territory of human development and achievement over millennia. His framework consists of five elements (quadrants, lines of intelligence, levels of development, states of awareness, and types) in which to position all categories of human knowledge and stages of human consciousness evolution, using the world's greatest traditions and their best aspects. Most of Wilber's books describe the basic tenets of Integral vision in greater or lesser detail; for example, the first 32 pages of *Integral Spirituality* (2006) set out a comprehensive yet accessible overview of the Integral approach. Wilber acknowledges that he has not devised a new philosophy or new body of human knowledge; he describes his contribution as that of a *map-maker*, offering a way of seeing that is extraordinarily layered and multidimensional, and which positions the many "truths" that constitute perspectives of reality. His intention with Integral mapping is "to honour and embrace every legitimate aspect of human consciousness" (Wilber, 2000: 2).

For AMSA to create a change strategy with common purpose, the leaders needed a coherent map for a territory that suffered constantly from being broken into pieces, with the tendency for each piece to be treated in isolation. Integral vision enables this kind of mapping, being a multi-dimensional approach – a meta-theory yet capable of versatile practical application. A key strategy of this intervention with the ExCo was to introduce an accessible practice derived from Ken Wilber's Integral Operating System, capable of keeping three focuses in play: ongoing diagnosis of the current situation; planning iterations of the way forward;

and monitoring and evaluating the implementation process. The Integral Operating System is also known as AQAL – acronym for the meta-theory which embraces the five key elements: all quadrants, all lines, all levels, all states, all types. This book focuses on the application of the foundational element, the quadrants.

It has been observed that in spite of the useful content of many excellent books on change management over the last 50 years,

> the managerial capacity to implement it has been woefully underdeveloped. In fact, instead of strengthening managers' ability to manage change, we've allowed managers to outsource change management to HR specialists and consultants instead of taking accountability themselves – an approach that often doesn't work.
>
> (Ashkenas, 2013: 1)

This underdeveloped capacity is inevitably not just about managing better business processes, but more importantly, about better ways of relating across levels and functions in implementing change processes.

Change affects *people* – whether it is adjusting a company's bottom-line focus, a rethink of company values, adjusting performance criteria, or managing individual behaviours. Accordingly, leaders need a way of anticipating how proposed changes may have an impact not only on strategy, outputs, and profits, but also on individuals and teams at every level. What might employees be required to do differently? And how do employees as individuals feel about the impending changes? Crucially, leaders need to be able to reflect on *themselves* in the process: What do I anticipate; how do I feel; what do I need to do in order to effectively lead the changes; who should I be connecting with as my support; how should I engage with resistance; and how can I prepare HR and our legal teams for the successful roll-out of new policies, strategies and performance criteria?

The dance of the quadrants

As a multi-dimensional approach, the Integral quadrants make sure that every element and angle of the client's reality is explored – subjective experience, worldview, personal values, objective contexts, actions, behaviours, and relationship dimensions. As Wilber (2001b: 243) says, "Consciousness is a four-quadrant affair, and it exists, if it exists at all, distributed across all four quadrants, anchored equally in each." The multiple perspectives help a leader and their team firstly to explore and map the current territory as accurately as possible; secondly, to plot the necessary calibrated adjustments; and lastly, to design how to put new processes into practice to reach the desired outcomes in each dimension of the system in which they find themselves.

In an immediate way, nothing could be more obvious, more within our grasp, than the meaning of the four quadrants – because each of us exists within all four perspectives, every second of every day:

- *Individual interior (upper-left quadrant)*: As an individual at work, there is my inner self, the space of thoughts, feelings, hopes, and fears that no one would know about unless you talked to me.
- *Individual exterior (upper-right quadrant)*: Then there is my objective being – the way I show up in my behaviours, in my body, in how I demonstrate my management style, in my skills.
- *Collective interior (lower-left quadrant)*: Then there are the people I relate to at work – my team and colleagues, who ideally share with me an intersubjective space of values, beliefs, concerns, and agreements on the right way to do things for the business.
- *Collective exterior (lower-right quadrant)*: Finally, there is the business – the inter-objective space of the systems, policies, and practices that deliver on its purpose.

There is simply no individual alive who is not interacting with all four of these domains all the time. Each quadrant, while irreducible to the others, intimately connects with and affects the other three – for better or worse. One of the most accessible explanations of Integral mapping can be found in Wilber (1998), and a brief but thorough introduction to the quadrants, and the significance of their interconnections, can be found in Wilber (2001b).

The quadrants as a diagnostic tool

The first stage of the work with AMSA, agreed with the MD, was to be a series of individual coaching sessions over six months with him and each member of the ExCo, after which the impact of the coaching would be assessed. This process included a self-assessment, and a 360° assessment of the quality of relationships and the efficiency of systems and processes for which each ExCo member was responsible.

Prior to the coaching, however, a two-day breakaway was held with the MD and his four ExCo members to create a cultural "audit" of the territory and to set the scope of the intervention. It was clear that the five ExCo members needed to spend some time in raising underlying issues with one another before we could establish the way forward. A further aim of this session was to familiarise the ExCo with the four perspectives of the Integral quadrants as we mapped the issues that were raised (see Figure 1.1).

Initially, halfway through Day One, the executives were frustrated because they imagined the purpose of the day was to walk out with a clear idea of strategy. It took them a while to accept that they were nowhere near being able to have that conversation – they needed to understand different members' needs and frustrations first, and then appreciate where each fitted into driving an overall strategy, but only when they all arrived at a shared understanding of their vision.

As the two days progressed, each of the participants populated their own four-quadrant flipchart which was displayed on a wall.

	Interior	Exterior
Individual	"I" – the inner world of the individual coaching client, e.g. beliefs, feelings, hopes, fears.	"It" – the manifestation of the individual coaching client through behaviour, dress, management style, etc.
Collective	"We" – the internal world of the client organisation, e.g. our shared cultural values, how we relate, what we intend.	"Its" – the external world of the client organisation, e.g. structures, systems, processes, outputs, measurable outcomes.

Figure 1.1 The coaching project within the Integral model. Source: Adapted from Aiken (2009: 37), adapted from Wilber (2001a: 65).

In summary, the Integral quadrants enable firstly *diagnosing* the current situation; secondly, *planning* the way forward; and thirdly, *monitoring and evaluating* progress.

Before we could begin the diagnosing and planning, however, we discovered that there were several frustrations among the five ExCo members that needed to be surfaced, frustrations that stood in the way of them listening to one another:

- There was a breakdown of trust between the head of Operations and the head of Investment Services Support, the former citing "constant scope creep" – projects did not come in on time or within budget.
- The head of Asset Management complained of his ExCo colleagues' missed opportunities to grow the business.
- The MD was angry with Human Resources for "dragging their heels" in advertising for and setting up new appointments, perceived as resistance to the non-negotiable commitment to black empowerment.

Evident was the poor quality of attention each member of the ExCo gave to one another. Interruptions were continuous, and tempers rose. The head of Marketing and Branding withdrew into silence. The MD tried to discourage personal jibes by himself resorting to personal jibes – wittier than most, but hardly encouraging anyone in the room to think well. At this first important meeting, some ground rules needed to be set to manage the group's inputs. The significance of these ground rules is detailed in Chapter 6 on establishing a listening culture. Suffice to say that a key agreement was that "Each speaks once before anybody speaks twice; and *no one is interrupted*" (see Kline, 1999: 102–103 for guidelines). Each member of the ExCo, starting with the MD, was given an equal amount of time to reflect on particular questions relating to each of the four quadrants, and to then populate each quadrant on their own flipchart with their thoughts.

The upper-left quadrant – my internal landscape

The domain of the individual interior in the upper-left quadrant includes the following aspects of experience and consciousness:

- My experiences, my beliefs, my consciousness, my values.
- What is meaningful to me, what I want and long for.
- My interpretation of the thoughts, feelings that arise in my body; the meaning I attach to them.
- My subjective truth (Divine, 2009: 24).

Each member of ExCo was asked to explain to his colleagues his key intentions, hopes, fears, and beliefs in undertaking his role. These thoughts were written up in the *upper-left* of the four quadrants set out on a flipchart. This quadrant represents an individual's *subjective being*, an individual's *subjective inner world* – feelings, hopes, beliefs, dreams, and fears. These are *internal* processes that mill about in one's mind, unknown by anyone unless a person chooses to disclose what he thinks, feels, values, and believes. The following kinds of question were asked, specifically with reference to the transformation project (see Figure 1.2):

- What values do you bring to your role?
- How do you feel about your leadership?
- What is your biggest hope going forward?
- What is your biggest fear?

The upper-right quadrant – how I show up

The domain of the individual exterior in the upper-right quadrant includes the following aspects of body and behaviour:

- Measurable part of our bodies: physical, neurological, biological, bio-energetic, skeletal, etc.
- Behavioural, observable actions: what I do.
- Measurable "doings": what I get done (Divine, 2009: 24).

	Interior	*Exterior*
Individual	**Upper-left quadrant: The subjective individual – their inner world:** • What values do you bring to your role? • How do you feel about your leadership? • What is your biggest hope going forward? • What is your biggest fear?	**Upper-right quadrant: The objective individual – their behaviour, physical presence:** • How would you describe your management style? • What skills are you most proud of? • Where would you focus on increasing your skills? • How do you think your staff see you as leader? • What do you see as your role in the success of these change projects/your strategy?
Collective	**Lower-left quadrant: Inter-subjective reality – shared world of values, beliefs, aspirations:** • What do you most value in each of your ExCo colleagues? • What do you most need from each of your ExCo colleagues going forward? • What behaviour/s would you most like your colleagues to change/be aware of? • What are the values that you believe you should be sharing to drive this transformation project/our strategy?	**Lower-right quadrant: Inter-objective reality – systems, policies, processes, outcomes:** • On a scale of 1 to 10, how would you rate the overall efficiencies of your systems and processes? • What interconnected systems and networks are you part of? • What aspects are working well? • What aspects are not working well? • What do you hope will be the main benefit/outcome of this transformation effort/meeting?

Figure 1.2 The quadrant questions posed in this chapter.

Wilber points out that we cannot have a mind without a body. A second domain – the *upper-right quadrant* – represents the way an individual shows up objectively through actions and behaviours, and includes their observable physical presence – including blood pressure and heart beat. Each ExCo member described for this quadrant his preferred management style, his way of doing, including his core skills, and even his dress code and awareness of his physical being. The following kinds of question were asked (see Figure 1.2):

• How would you describe your management style?
• What skills are you most proud of?
• Where would you focus on increasing your skills?
• How do you think your staff see you as leader?
• What do you see as your role in the success of these three change projects?

The lower-left quadrant – our shared internal world

The domain of the collective interior in the lower-left quadrant includes the following aspects of culture and relationships:

- Relationships, community, "we" domains.
- Being part of a shared sense of reality, rightness, cohesion, belonging.
- Cultural mores, norms, rituals, traditions that "we" share.
- Shared language, symbols, meaning.
- Unspoken rules that "we" understand (Divine, 2009: 24).

The lower-left quadrant is the *inter-subjective internal world of the collective* – our shared values, how we relate, what we intend. As Bennis (2007: 3–4) affirms: "Leadership is grounded in a relationship. In its simplest form, it is a tripod – a leader or leaders, followers, and the common goal they want to achieve. None of those three elements can survive without the others." Each member of AMSA's ExCo reflected on which relationships supported their intentions and actions, and which detracted, as well as what was common to their values and vision as ExCo. It is worth considering what makes a *relationship*. It is more than just standing next to someone you recognise as a colleague at the coffee machine. Consider what makes "we" more powerful than just "I": our shared experience or shared values, our mutuality. The following kinds of question were asked (see Figure 1.2):

- What do you most value in each of your ExCo colleagues?
- What do you most need from each of your ExCo colleagues going forward?
- What behaviour/s would you most like your colleagues to change/be aware of?
- What are the values that you believe you should be sharing to drive this transformation project?

The lower-right quadrant – our objective world

The domain of the collective exterior in the lower-right quadrant includes the following aspects of structures and systems:

- Measurable aspects of the collective domain: What "we" do, the results of our performance, how we get things done.
- Frameworks and structures for planning, designing, analysing, organising, monitoring.
- Systems, theories, processes, sciences (what, how things work and why, based on facts, measurements, and analysis).
- Environment/physical world: both human-made structures and nature (Divine, 2009: 24).

The lower-right quadrant is the visible mark that the collective makes in the physical world. This fourth domain is *the objective collective world of evidential contexts, outputs, systems, and structures*. The architecture and layout of the building, or where people sit, for example, can impact on individuals and behaviours, as can policies, legal frameworks, systems of reward, business practices, and their outputs. These are the material manifestation of the aspirations and intentions of the collective. At this session, the *structures and outcomes* of the three enabling culture projects were mapped in this lower-right quadrant. The following kinds of question were asked (see Figure 1.2):

- On a scale of 1 to 10, how would you rate the overall efficiencies of your systems and processes?
- What interconnected systems and networks are you part of?
- What aspects are working well?
- What aspects are not working well?
- What do you hope will be the main benefit of this transformation effort?

Results of the dance of the quadrants

The outcome of this first round of reflections using the quadrants was that some negative judgments of one another were replaced with a deeper understanding of the challenges faced by individual colleagues responsible for different areas in AMSA. In the next round, each of the five participants reflected further on their individual interpretation and understanding of their role as senior manager in implementing the three transformation projects. They also compared and refined their joint understanding of the values and intentions of the three projects in relation to the desired organisational culture and, finally, set out the systemic context – enablers of the projects in terms of policies, practices, communication processes, and hoped-for improved outputs.

A further outcome of these fresh insights was a commitment from the ExCo members to initiate more frequent cross-functional communications and alliances across their respective divisions, a decision which, as will unfold in future chapters, percolated to their direct reports, and eventually to entire teams within each division. Leading on from this initial intervention with the Executive Committee, a pattern of consultation, one-on-one coaching, teamwork and workshop facilitation over a two-year period began to emerge as a series of developmental cycles in transforming the organisational culture. A vital component of my interaction with the ExCo over this period was skills transfer – their learning to lead with coaching competencies.

Conclusion

The intention in this chapter has been to introduce the power of the Integral quadrants as a diagnostic process, as a way of revealing the layers in a current situation, and enabling individuals to reflect on personal values, hopes, and fears. As the chapters unfold, the versatility of the quadrants in mapping and disclosing a variety of issues that emerged at AMSA and elsewhere is demonstrated. Chapter 2 explains a critical concept in Integral theory, that of *holons*, as well as exploring "sweet spots" and "blind spots" in coaching one-on-one with the quadrants.

Chapter 2

Sweet spots and blind spots

Parts and wholes, parts in wholes

Key to the success of the kind of transformation projects described in Chapter 1 is the significance for leaders of the concept of *holons* and *holarchies*. "To understand the whole, it is necessary to understand the parts. To understand the parts, it is necessary to understand the whole. Such is the circle of understanding," says Wilber (2001b: 1). In 1926, Jan Smuts gave us the truism that "the whole is more than the sum of its parts" (Smuts, 2013). Arthur Koestler expanded on this observation in his quest to understand the *interaction* between parts and wholes. He coined the term *holon* to describe a whole which is simultaneously a part *and* a whole, and *holarchy* to represent an entire living system, a system made up of interacting holons (Edwards, 2003).

A child is an individual holon – a *whole* – and at the same time *part* of a nuclear family, itself a holon. An essential concept that Wilber greatly expanded was Koestler's insight that there are different levels of operation in any one holon: a child of 3, for example, operates at a simpler level of complexity than a sibling of 12; and their parents or carers typically would be functioning at increasingly greater levels of complexity. The main point is that nothing in a living system exists on its own. An organisation is a living system. Everything connects and contributes to the whole *at its own level*, for better or worse. What matters is the skill of evaluating each part's contribution as a part of the bigger holon.

Dominator hierarchies versus natural hierarchies

A holarchy is another word for a functioning *hierarchy*. There is considerable literature on the role of hierarchies in organisations, including the pros and cons of flattening hierarchies in the interests of greater productivity (see for example Alston, Alston, and Mueller, 2020). Wilber makes a critical distinction between the essential qualities and values of a *dominator (or pathological) hierarchy* and those of a *natural hierarchy* (see Wilber, 2001b: 67–68). The traditional school system is an example of a dominator hierarchy. Pupils are under the control of teachers and prefects, who are under the control of the principal, who is dominated

DOI: 10.4324/9781003377221-3

by the school's board of directors who take their lead from the Department of Education, and so on. The authority and decision-makers flow from the top down, with very little or no influence on the system from the bottom up. In a dominator hierarchy, the position or level a person occupies determines the degree of power and status they have – but says nothing about the *quality of relationship* that might exist up and down the line. How often have we heard the "dominator-hierarchy" complaint about managers having been promoted or awarded bonuses for goal achievement while wreaking havoc in the lives of the people who report to them? Tera Allas and Bill Schaninger write in their article "The Boss Factor: Making the World a Better Place through Workplace Relationships":

> Unfortunately, research also shows that most people find their managers to be far from ideal; for example, in a recent survey, 75 per cent of survey participants said that the most stressful aspect of their job was their immediate boss. And those describing very bad and quite bad relationships with management reported substantially lower job satisfaction than those with very good and quite good relationships.
>
> (Allas and Schaninger, 2020: 2)

An example of a *natural hierarchy* is your body. Imagine that the smallest holon is an atom (there are smaller …). When a single atom interacts with other atoms, they form a more complex, higher-functioning holon, a molecule. A molecule integrates with other molecules to form a cell; cells integrate with more cells to form tissues; and tissues differentiate to become organs to perform particular functions – like a bladder, a heart, a stomach. All the organs at ever-greater levels of complexity in their functioning are integrated into the whole living system, the human body. In a natural hierarchy, every holon in the system is in communication with and is affected by other holons (Wilber, 2000a: 20–27). Damage to holons in one part of the body has the potential to harm many other parts of the living system – as we are beginning to discover with the microbiome in our gut. Giulia Enders (2015), for example, describes the powerful consequences of interactions in our body in her best-selling book *Gut: The Inside Story of Our Body's Most Under-rated Organ*.

Nature is a living system, a natural hierarchy of interacting holons, the stability and health of which are seriously affected by certain human interventions – examples include the various impacts of deforestation, the destructive build-up of plastic waste in our oceans, and the effects on our atmosphere of burning fossil fuels. We have been slow learners in recognising that we interfere in the self-organising processes of a living system at our peril – climate change and the COVID-19 pandemic are two bruising cases in point. They show that the action of an individual, for good or ill, can rapidly escalate in its effect on groups, on institutions, on whole countries and nations, and even on our planet. And now, there is an emergent but significant recognition that formal and informal organisations, and their systems and structures of governance, would thrive and prosper more as natural hierarchies, living systems which recognise and are constantly in flow with all the moving parts, from the simplest to the most complex. The critical part of this recognition is the awareness of the role that leaders play in determining the health of every other holon in the system.

Apply this concept of holons to the overall structure and functioning of an organisation like AMSA. At the top sits a *high-level holon* consisting of the MD and his four senior managers. The terms *high*, *medium*, and *low* refer to levels of operational complexity, not superiority versus inferiority. "High-level" in the context of Integral vision means operating with an expected advanced degree of complexity, reflective awareness, and resilience. Four *medium-level holons* are represented by AMSA's four divisions: Services, Investments, Marketing, and Operations – "medium", that is, in comparison with the more complex demands for managing at ExCo level. These in turn are populated with *lower-level holons* – the teams individually responsible for differentiated functions within each of the divisions, but not for overseeing the complexity of the whole interconnected system. At the start of the transformation project with AMSA, the climate in the organisation was one of distrust and disconnection from the bottom up (lower-level and medium-level holons), as the leadership tried to enforce compliance and better performance for all the right reasons, from the top down (high-level holon). What was missing was a healthy relationship among the holons: a vigorous exchange of opinions and ideas among all the moving parts in the organisation, guided by co-created agreement on non-negotiable shared values and common purpose – and the managerial capacity to implement this.

Coaching individuals with the quadrants

At the group ExCo breakaway described in Chapter 1, we used the quadrants to diagnose the current situation facing each executive in implementing AMSA's transformation initiatives. The next stage was the individual coaching sessions over six months with each ExCo member. We began the series of coaching sessions for each individual by reviewing his quadrant flipchart from the breakaway. The purpose of these coaching sessions was firstly to raise reflective self-awareness of each of the four quadrants in each member of ExCo, in order to individually tailor their actions and interactions over the next six months to meet the transformation objectives of the three overlapping projects. Landrum and Gardner (2005: 254) affirm the validity of this approach:

> An Integrally informed approach to strategic change would begin change at the inner individual level, the primary quadrant, but would continue effecting change through all four quadrants. Change can only be effective, evolving, and eternal if implemented and incorporated in all quadrants and at all levels.

Eric's coaching journey

Eric headed up Operations. Think of Eric as a high-level holon, and Operations as the holarchy for which he is responsible. In his late 40s, he showed a deep-seated need for affirmation in the disclosures made in the breakaway session. He was conscientious and rigorous in his attention to detail. He also, by his own admission, had a very low uncertainty threshold. His comments regarding his interactions with his ExCo colleagues were mostly negative. The two extremes – his judgmental tendencies and his need for affirmation – kept him in an agonising turmoil when we first met, literally agonising: his first open criticisms of leadership and strategy to the managing director and his colleagues at our breakaway resulted in severe stomach pain. Here is a sample from a transcript of one of Eric's first coaching sessions, reflecting on his stomach ache and the need to be perfect:

D: What are you assuming are the consequences for not being perfect?
E: I told you this before, I think. My whole, the whole Afrikaner life is about – "What would people say?" And I think perfectionism is a very good defence mechanism to make sure that what people would say – they would say only the good things, not the bad things. So, in essence, once again it boils down to me living my life for other people. And it's stupid, because if my car is dirty why should it bother other people? Do you understand what I'm saying? But it bothers me.
D: When does it go too far?
E: I think that the day I was born it went too far. And it just got worse, because that's the culture I was born into.

(Aiken, 2009: 109)

In time, he affirmed that having this coaching time to be listened to, even if challenging, gave him more and more courage to care less about needing the good opinion of others. While that was a gain for him, his deeply negative assumptions about races and religions other than his own not only raised serious ethical dilemmas, but were obstacles to his leadership potential in AMSA's cultural transformation project. Here is another excerpt from his coaching transcript:

E: I've got expectations on what needs to be delivered. And what does Aaron [his ExCo colleague] do? He starts changing the goalposts. In other words, he starts to tell me that my expectations are unrealistic. And then I go back and I say, "Aaron, we agreed. We agreed to these things in the project scoping documents. How come now that I'm insisting that this must be delivered because I am the business owner, you're asking me would I expect this from another vendor? Why are we going there? Why didn't you ask that six months ago when we put that down?"
   Aaron has gotten away with murder of non-delivery since that day he walked in here. And you are going to call me a racist now as far as people from his religion are concerned, but let me share a little story with you. My whole life experience with these people has been that they are duckers and divers, and I've told you that before. And they will do everything just to look after themselves, even at the expense of other people. Now this is my take on it.

(Aiken, 2009: 107)

Through a lifetime of habit, Eric interpreted circumstances through very constrained lenses. Most of his life, his preferred way had worked for him. In this rapidly changing world of work in which he was mandated to help lead the change, he was experiencing extreme stress as the limits of his worldview came under fire. One of his coaching challenges was to expand the range of his vision.

Quadrant sweet spots and blind spots

A first step in the individual coaching sessions was for each ExCo member to recognise their personal quadrant "sweet spots" and "blind spots" – a pattern that each identified for themselves. The quadrants enable a balanced look at a project, a person, or a situation, taking all four lenses into account, as demonstrated in Chapter 1. Added to this, as individuals, we tend to have a particular preference for viewing life predominantly through one or two of the quadrants (see Figure 2.1). The late Laura Divine of Integral Coaching Canada Inc., with whom I have studied, has written an exquisite description of particular quadrant preferences and their consequences (Divine, 2009).

	Interior	Exterior
Individual	**Upper-left quadrant – my inner world** I see and relate from a place of personal meaning and values – my views, feelings, thoughts, what I most care about.	**Upper-right quadrant – my behaviour** I focus on and relate to action, to doing; I value what gets done, task completion.
Collective	**Lower-left quadrant – shared world** I relate to shared meaning, belonging and inclusion, shared understanding, connection.	**Lower-right quadrant – systems** I see and relate to the system, how it all fits together (goals, processes, roles, and structures), and how it supports and enables.

Figure 2.1 Quadrant preferences. Source: Adapted from Divine (2009: 27).

When we understand a person's preferred view of the world through a favoured quadrant, we can look out at the world as that person sees it. We develop insight into what someone might be missing by not paying equal attention to the view from other quadrant lenses. For example, Eric's sweet spot was the *upper-right quadrant* – just get going and *do* things, pay attention to detail and get it right; live by the correct rules. He was the perfect person for operational focus.

One of his blind spots, however, was the view from the *lower-right quadrant*: being able to stand back and see the bigger picture, taking the time to understand how patterns beyond his own immediate concern fit together. Another blind spot for Eric was the *lower-left quadrant*: in this interpersonal space, he did not much care how other people were affected by negative interactions with him, including his family. It was no surprise that he was resistant as a leader to acquiring coaching skills. Daniel Goleman, in his research on six leadership styles, suggests that the awareness of each style and its particular usefulness and limitations would add considerable skill to the emotionally intelligent leader. He claims that:

> Of the six styles, our research found that the coaching style is used least often. Many leaders told us they don't have the time in this high-pressure economy for the slow and tedious work of teaching people and helping them grow.
>
> (Goleman, 2000: 87)

As long as the people for whom Eric was responsible (especially his two daughters) were living according to his rules, life was rosy. A crisis in his relationship with his elder daughter eventually led to a major breakthrough for Eric in his leadership style at work.

When Eric came home from work each day, he looked forward to seeing his wife and his two girls waiting to greet him at the door linking the garage to the house. His elder daughter, then in her final school year, had recently fallen out with her father when she told him she wanted to stay in digs when she started university in the new year, and he had flatly refused his permission. She stopped appearing at the door with her mother and sister to greet him each day on his return home from work, and the two of them stopped speaking to each other altogether. It was the first time this kind of disruption with his daughter had ever happened, and Eric was alternately angry at her defiance and distraught at losing access to a close and loving relationship. As the day neared when she would leave to start university – she was adamant that she would leave home whatever the consequences – he told me this story, saying how upset he was that she still didn't speak to him. I asked if he had tried to speak to her, and he looked at me aghast. That would be against his rules: she was in the wrong, she should be obedient to his wishes, and she must apologise to him. "And if she doesn't?" I asked. He changed the subject.

Two weeks later, Eric started our session by reminding me of the on-the-job practices he had agreed to undertake in exploring his sweet spots and blind spots on the quadrants. His first experiment was setting up a meeting with his "nemesis",

Aaron. His practice was to focus on his much-neglected lower-left quadrant, the place of shared values, of relationship, by paying positive attention in listening to Aaron's reasons for changing agreements, instead of just criticising him. Aaron's sweet spot was Eric's second blind spot, the lower-right quadrant: the world of systems, processes, understanding how things fit together.

Eric came away from that discussion with a better understanding of Aaron's occasional need to shift timelines and reframe projects that Eric thought had been cast in stone. Aaron looked at multiple streams of data for changing patterns in the system, constantly adjusting the facts and the figures according to his research. For the first time in their working together, Eric conceded that Aaron's prevaricating stemmed from his desire to do the best job he could in shifting circumstances. He was still not entirely forgiving of Aaron's upper-right quadrant blind spot – his failure to act on time, to get things done. The best part of Eric's story, however, was what happened later that week.

As he pulled his car into the garage at home and caught sight of his wife and his younger daughter, he decided, with his stomach in a painful knot, that he would invite his elder daughter to talk to him "from her heart", that he would promise just to listen, as he had with Aaron. When she realised he was not going to rage and judge her, that he genuinely wanted to listen to her, she told him her reasons for wanting to leave home and live in digs – "Good reasons", he said, "what I had wanted for myself at her age." It was a moving moment for both of them, indeed for the family.

Eric's big realisation at work was the need to suspend judgment and be willing first to listen as a leader in a stressed environment. Working actively with one's quadrant

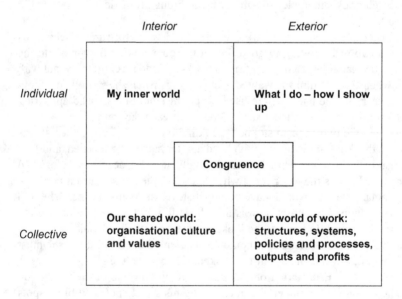

Figure 2.2 The ideal: congruence.

blind spots is an excellent step towards "both-and", "true-but-partial" perspective-taking, rather than Eric's rigid "either-or" approach. The ideal is congruence among the four quadrants (see Figure 2.2), bearing in mind that they are in a constant state of flux in relation to one another. It is therefore good practice, especially when new projects are underway, to revisit each quadrant frequently, checking for alignment.

In Chapter 3, a senior manager, who is aiming at a longed-for promotion, is guided by the quadrants to greater self-awareness in order to increase her relational effectiveness.

Chapter 3

A four-quadrant coaching conversation

Melinda: A journey of hope

Melinda was a financial manager in an Operations section. She was in line for the promotion that she believed she deserved, and on which she had set her heart. However, while her performance in her role was rated highly, there were complaints about her erratic and volatile behaviour with staff. Promotion would mean management of a bigger team than her current one, and her behaviour was therefore seen as a concern by her line manager. Since coaching for senior staff was encouraged, Melinda requested a period of coaching for the six months leading up to her next performance appraisal, at which time there would be 360° feedback on her performance and behaviour patterns.

Using the four quadrants to plot a coaching conversation

On the surface, Melinda came across as supremely confident, and professed herself slightly puzzled by complaints about her behaviour. When she spoke, she leaned forward and accompanied her comments with firm hand gestures and assertive nods as she confirmed her reasons for wanting "to experience coaching". The bottom line was that she saw my role as helping to convince her line manager that she was deserving of promotion. *Her* role was to clarify to me what she actually did. She sat back decisively: it was my turn to speak. I began by describing the reasons her company was engaging with coaching, that it was an opportunity for managers and team leaders to grow their awareness of their own management style and find opportunities to expand their relational skills, apart from their technical know-how. This had become a focus, I explained, because of the recognition by the senior leadership that performance excellence could be enhanced by how people felt they were treated on the job. Melinda looked at me askance. I said that not only might she understand her own motivations better through our sessions; she might also achieve even more excellence from her team if she were more aware of her interactions with them. Furthermore, I added, a hoped-for outcome of her experience of coaching would be the transfer of coaching skills to her as part of her management competencies.

DOI: 10.4324/9781003377221-4

"Me? A coach?" Melinda laughed, then said seriously, "I don't come to work to make people feel nice – we are here to get results for the business, and I make sure we do that, whether people like me or not."

"So tell me about you at work – what do you value most?" I cut away from being drawn into a dispute with her on the merits of coaching as a leadership style, to exploring her inner world (in "quadrant-speak", the upper-left quadrant space of values, hopes, ambitions, dreams, beliefs, and fears). Melinda started to draw a picture of someone who lived for her work, for the reward of success. She declared hard work to be praiseworthy and achievement rewarding for its own sake, though having it acknowledged was also very important. She described herself as a divorced, single mother of two teenagers. Her way of coping with the pressures of work and family life was to be disciplined and structured. She readily volunteered that her approach to life caused conflict between her and her 16-year-old daughter, and laughingly mimicked her daughter complaining, "We're not in the army, you know."

I asked her what this potential promotion would mean for her. More money would be good, she said, but even more rewarding would be the acknowledgement that she deserved the extra responsibility of an expanded management role. "I'm ready for it," she said, "I *know* I have the right skills." And if she was passed over for promotion … ? I watched her body language as she slumped momentarily, then sat erect again, asserting brightly, "That's not going to happen, is it?"

"So what are the right skills?" I asked, moving attention from Melinda's subjective being to the way she showed up objectively (the upper-right quadrant of individual skills, behaviours, management style, physical being). Apart from her technical competencies, she described the skill of being able to keep her finger on several pulses simultaneously. She admitted she "didn't suffer fools gladly" and I asked her how that showed up. "Look," she said after a moment, "when someone needs a *klap* [slap] over the earhole, I give it to them – verbally, you realise. They might not like me for it, but I get results."

I moved on to what mattered to Melinda in terms of relationships and shared values – the lower-left quadrant. "If you think back on anyone who helped you become the person you are proud to be today, who was (or is) that person to you, and what was (or is) special about their impact on you?" Melinda didn't hesitate: "My mum." She told me her mother died of cancer when Melinda was 17, not long after she knew her daughter had passed her final school exams with distinction. "So, what was your mother like?" I asked. Melinda said, "She thought the sun shone out of me. I could do no wrong in her eyes – even when I was wrong. I think I am who I am today because I never want to disappoint her – even now." I noted this little nugget about the quality of relationship between Melinda and her mother, planning to make use of these tender recollections when there was a more deeply established basis of trust between us.

Before we wrapped up our first session, I wanted to know who would be important to Melinda in achieving her promotion. Melinda was thoughtful for a few moments before acknowledging her line manager, without whose support nothing would change. She also spoke of peers encouraging her to work with them in a more influential capacity. I also asked who she thought might stand in the way. Melinda scowled. "There's only one person whom I know bad-mouths me to anyone who will listen, including my manager – Jenny!"

In navigating this first session by means of the quadrants, the intention had been to learn as much as I could about Melinda, while encouraging and building on her underused capacity to both self-reflect (upper-left quadrant) and reflect on others (lower-left quadrant). Two conditions of our coaching sessions, already contracted, were that Melinda would keep a journal and that coaching entailed a commitment to "homework". I had explained that while every single coaching session was important in itself, even more important was what she was aware of between sessions.

Melinda's "homework" for our next session was to bring her reflections on the relationship with Jenny: in her view, what worked, and what didn't work. In closing, I asked her what she had enjoyed, if anything, about the session. After a short silence, she said "I didn't think this was coaching. I just was able to talk about some things because you asked me." She fell silent, looking at me almost with suspicion, as if I had tricked her into talking. "Anyway," she said, standing up abruptly, "I am looking forward to what you think I can do about Jenny." I thanked her, affirming her for what she had shared so far, and confirmed that I too was looking forward to next time.

Melinda's sweet spots were the lower-right quadrant and upper-right quadrant – thinking about the best way to serve the system, and then getting things done. Her blind spots, her self-awareness (upper-left quadrant) and relational awareness (lower-left quadrant), had been largely the focus of this first session. In order for Melinda to meet the conditions for her promotion at her next performance appraisal, she would need to earn positive feedback from her team and her peers. Pamela McLean (2019: xx) asserts, "Today's leaders need to know themselves – their blind spots, values, possibilities, patterns, and old stories. They need to know how to be team players, to think and engage the collective leadership of those around them."

Making use of Daniel Goleman's model of four domains of emotional intelligence and their 12 competencies would require Melinda to develop her capacity for self-awareness, aligned with Wilber's upper-left quadrant, Melinda's inner subjective space. Originally a five-domain model (Goleman, 1996), the four-domain model was redesigned in 2002 and can be found in Goleman, Boyatzis, and McKee (2002: 325–332). The four-domain model with its 12 competencies is outlined in Figure 3.1, with the domains arranged in alignment with the four-quadrant structure of the Integral Operating System.

Once Melinda had more conscious awareness of the patterns that she needed to change, she would then need to self-manage in the moment, aligned with Wilber's upper-right quadrant – her behaviours. Hopefully, Melinda's relational awareness and sensitivity to managing others would come into focus – the lower-left quadrant of the Integral Operating System, the inter-subjective space of connection. And finally, there should be a measurable positive impact for the business – Wilber's lower-right quadrant of systems and outputs.

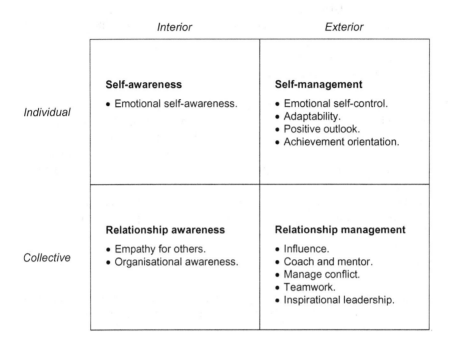

Figure 3.1 Goleman's model of emotional intelligence, aligned with the Integral quadrants. Source: Adapted from Goleman and Boyatzis (2017: 3).

We agreed for the next few weeks to keep her focus on the relationship with Jenny. Melinda's homework was to notice, just *notice*, every time she was in relation to Jenny. I stressed that I was not asking Melinda to get it right, not yet – just to notice and journal her *reactions in the moment*. "Try to remember," I urged, "that Jenny has her own baggage, influences in her life that you can't know about, and which you did not cause: patterns that cause her to have a knee-jerk reaction to you as much as your patterns cause your own knee-jerk reactions to her."

I include here a part of a transcription of our third session:

D: What have been your reflections since our last session?

M: Two things – I've been thinking about team complaints about me, and feeling frustrated that when I do fly off the handle, my line manager judges me and not the performance issues in my team. She sees only my lack of professional leadership, poor self-control.

D: Is that perception of you true?

M: Sometimes. It's not everyone that I have a problem with – it's Jenny who affects everyone. She is a difficult team member; she's a good worker but our relationship is complicated – we rub each other up the wrong way. She second-guesses me, tries things her own way after we've already agreed an approach.

It makes me mad. Her stubbornness means jobs have to be redone, it costs time which the team resents and blames me for – Jenny causes the others to gang up on me.

D: How does that make you feel?

M: When I'm under pressure I know I can overreact.

D: How do you react?

M: Sometimes people get offended by the way I speak to them. I think they deserve it at the time, especially Jenny when she deliberately goes ahead with what I believe we have specifically agreed she should not do. But then I have to spend days putting out fires, which impacts on team delivery and efficiency.

D: Frustrating for you. If you knew the only person you can change to get your promotion is *you*, what could you think of doing differently? You can't force Jenny to change, and your being abusive is obviously not changing anything. What if you change how you react to her? She might respond differently. What are your thoughts?

Melinda looked dubious. She was not prepared to drop standards to keep the peace.

D: What do you think Jenny is trying to prove when she goes about doing something her own way? You have admitted that sometimes her way works just as well …

M: But often it does not!

D: How often do you praise Jenny?

Melinda looked at me as if I had lost my mind.

The power of affirmations

I reminded Melinda of her mother, how she encouraged Melinda and made her feel so intelligent and valued, and asked her again, "What do you think Jenny is trying to do when she goes her own way? Even when she gets it wrong, what could you admire in her?" It took a while for Melinda to acknowledge that Jenny craved recognition for showing initiative.

Melinda's "homework" was now to try to recognise and affirm Jenny's efforts to be an independent thinker, even when there was a less-than-perfect outcome. The affirmation then needed to be followed up with getting Jenny to think of how she could have achieved a better outcome, instead of simply telling her – or rather yelling it at her. Melinda sighed as we ended the session, saying she did not have the time for all this "nurturing nonsense".

The next couple of weeks were difficult for Melinda, as she worked with both being self-aware and trying to modify her hostile reactions in the moment. Trying to be affirming when she just wanted to tear Jenny's head off was almost a step too far. She walked out of coaching in the first ten minutes of our fifth session, nearly three months into our coaching contract, vowing never to return, and I had a first-hand experience of her fiery temper and her highly expressive vocabulary. Paradoxically, this proved to be a good moment, a turning point. A fortnight later, after she requested that we continue with coaching, she explained her outburst: she was furious with me for her growing sense of feeling trapped. She now knew clearly that she had to change her reactions in the moment; but at the same time, she did not want to change. Her growing ability to observe herself *in the moment* forced the recognition that she was part of the problem in Jenny's aggressive relationship to her, but years of habit caused Melinda to resist – and resent – the discipline of reframing her reaction. The big gain, however, was that she was now able to see evidence of the impact of her behaviour on others from moment to moment, and was now conscious of *choosing* to moderate her responses. She recognised increasingly clearly that she played a key role in how others, like Jenny, behaved in *their* responses.

A necessary tension exists between the two upper quadrants representing the *individual (my way)* and the two lower quadrants representing the *collective or communal (our way)*. The power of mapping on these four quadrants reveals the extent to which an individual is in alignment with their values and intentions; their awareness of how they show up; their quality of connection in relating to others and to the organisational culture; and the way in which their actions support or undermine the system in the alignment of people, purpose, and performance. Melinda began to see the broken connection between her values and aspirations at work (upper-left quadrant) and how she showed up in her management style – critical, unforgiving, and abrasive (upper-right quadrant). She began to see the impact of giving affirmations for effort on generating positive relationships (lower-left quadrant), while not dropping her demand for standards required by the system (lower-right quadrant). She learned the power of following an appreciation for effort (short, relevant, and genuine) with good, open questions that prompted Jenny to find the very solutions Melinda wanted, for example: "Well done for trying. What do you think you would do now to get a better result? Who do you need to help you? When can we check in again?"

It was an uneven journey with two steps forward, one step back, as Melinda struggled to change her own habits in order to reframe what had been a confrontational relationship between her and Jenny to one of mutual co-operation. To begin with, she felt false, untruthful, when she first tried to affirm Jenny's efforts, and Jenny was very suspicious of Melinda's praise. A positive shift between them happened when Melinda made herself vulnerable to Jenny by acknowledging that she had been a harsh critic who seldom gave appreciations. She confessed to Jenny the positive impact appreciation from her mother had had on her, while always encouraging her to reach for excellence. The upshot before Melinda's performance appraisal was positive feedback in her 360° review, particularly from Jenny. I asked the MD for his perception of the changes in Melinda. He remarked:

It's difficult for me to comment from a distance. Obviously, we've seen this extraordinary – almost metamorphosis – of Melinda over the last couple of months … That's the big breakthrough here – everyone had been telling her about her behaviour, but she had resisted. I mean, I had that discussion with her. I said, "You won't be promoted until your behaviour reflects what I expect from a senior manager." Her manager had been saying that to her for ages before that, in very similar vein, but yet she had resisted. She said, "No, that would be giving up my individuality, and I'm not going to do it." So what was the real breakthrough? What persuaded her that it isn't asking her to give away her personality?

The "breakthrough", according to Melinda, was *affirmation* – not just affirmation for what she already knew she did very well (upper-right quadrant, the doing, the technical competencies) – but for her *being*. She didn't have to fight to be heard and believed. Consequently, she was willing to open up to the limitations in her current behaviours. Her ongoing journey, however, was not a perfect curve of increased awareness – she acknowledged regressions – but the significant difference between before and after coaching was her ability to recognise her patterns and choose to act differently. Through the practices she set herself, through small daily steps, and through journaling her observations, Melinda showed an increase on all four of the emotional intelligence quadrants: self-awareness, self-management, relational awareness, and relationship management (Goleman, Boyatzis, and McKee, 2002).

Avoiding back-sliding to default behaviour patterns

There is every likelihood when formal coaching sessions end, without the constant reminder to observe oneself, to commit to new practices and give reflective feedback, that the leader-manager finds themself defaulting to previous more deeply embedded patterns. There is increasing evidence of the benefit of continuous on-the-job support as part of workplace culture. Jennifer Garvey Berger recommends ongoing, regular, formal conversations about work, where leaders meet with direct reports to provide opportunities for appraisal and reflection, and creating personal space for self-reflection: "It enables us to ask questions about what we might learn from the specific situation, how we might do things differently, and how we might be different" (Garvey Berger, 2012: location 3113).

Chapter 4 illustrates how the quadrants play a role in distinguishing between "truthfulness", derived from an individual's subjective experience (upper-left quadrant), and "truth", an objective assessment of a range of factors (upper-right quadrant, lower-right quadrant). It is important to appreciate someone's experience as *truthful*, while enabling them to acknowledge their view as *partial*, especially in cultural conflict situations.

Chapter 4

True – but partial

"I am right, and I can prove it"

Two conflicting narratives collide

Two financial administrators at AMSA were in conflict with each other. The younger of the two, Phumla, a black woman in her mid-thirties and a skilled, experienced analyst, was on the point of handing in her resignation, blaming the person to whom she reported for making her life unbearable. Her manager, Jeanette, a white woman of 60, hotly refuted any adversarial behaviour, claiming the younger woman was trying to force her out of her job. Each blamed the other for racist behaviours – Phumla's perception of Jeanette was that she was a typical white racist, no matter how vehemently Jeanette denied this, and that Jeanette's behaviour clearly revealed her belief that "blacks are never good enough". Jeanette's perception, reinforced by some of her friends and colleagues, was that she was a victim of "reverse racism".

Imagine an exquisite yacht equipped to compete in a high-stakes around-the-world race through unpredictable seas – but manned with a conflicted crew, each of whom pulls in different directions. Each crew member has their own deep beliefs about how things happen and what should be done around here – not because each is simply being bloody-minded, but because each believes they have substantial evidence for, and experience of, what they hold to be true. Each individual crew member on the yacht has their own *discourse* or *narrative* about why acts, events, structures, and thoughts should occur as they do. AMSA was just such a discursive terrain, crisscrossed with conflicting viewpoints.

Sociological critical discourse theory enables participants to understand the ways in which identities (and exclusions) are socially constructed and fluid. Critical discourse theory helps us understand the impact of history, social forces, political power, and economic power in shaping the diverse stories we tell ourselves – discursive terrains – the way our identities are constructed.

What are *discursive terrains*? Organisations and their members or employees exist in sociocultural spaces. A sociocultural space like AMSA is crosscut by a multiplicity of discourses that exist simultaneously within that space at any one time. A constant challenge for coach and leader is that the discursive territory is not static – it is like a bundle of variegated, twisted embroidery threads, each thread

DOI: 10.4324/9781003377221-5

representing a particular group, constantly weaving and transforming. The upside is that meaning-making in sociocultural spaces is not rigid. Like osmosis, in the presence of the appropriate conditions differing groups can influence one another and reconstitute as a united group of shared concerns, shared practices, and shared values (Steyn, 2001: 107–136).

Six contested themes

From individual interviews and focus groups, six contested themes (or *discursive terrains*) were in play at AMSA. Each of these themes was cross-referenced with verbal occurrences among particular groups in South Africa noted in the media, in transcripts, and in academic research (Aiken, 2009). Phumla's experience and assumptions echoed a recurring theme among black staff at AMSA: "*Scratch a white and you will find a racist.*" There was evidence of deep wounding on the part of those designated "non-white" under apartheid, particularly among black African staff, as opposed to mixed-race ("coloured") and Indian staff. The deepest wound was inevitably to self-esteem. For those living with unresolved and unacknowledged wounds, it did not take much to trigger painful assumptions based on previous actual life experiences, as in Phumla's case.

A second recurring theme is best described through Phumla's story of being undermined, micromanaged, and patronised by her manager. Jeanette had set herself the positive intention to help Phumla develop as a member of her team. Her way was to surreptitiously check Phumla's work, thinking Phumla wouldn't notice, and sometimes make alterations to Phumla's reports without referring them back to her or openly pointing out corrections. Phumla was excluded from directly receiving information from her internal clients, because Jeanette ensured that she filtered it before conveying it to Phumla. Jeanette's management and mentoring of Phumla in her role typified the "kindly" but unexamined assumption of *deficit performance* in the black African group ("*How can they know any better?*") by particularly (but not exclusively) the white group.

Jeanette's responses to Phumla illustrated a third recurring theme: "*We're the victims of reverse racism!*" Despite everything Jeanette thought she was doing to help her, she believed that Phumla's hostile behaviour was driven by wanting Jeanette removed from her job and taking it for herself – and Jeanette felt increasingly angry about and silenced by AMSA's commitment to black empowerment.

Jeanette's grievance was reinforced by Eric (whom we met in Chapter 2), who demonstrated a fourth theme that recurred in interviews at AMSA: a predisposition to use a negative generalisation about a particular group to explain the specific behaviour or actions of one individual – "*All [Jews/Muslims/blacks/whites/gays/women/Greeks] behave like this.*" Thus, a pre-existing untrue limiting assumption regarding a particular group pre-empted an objective appraisal of an individual within that group. An action that might have been regarded as due to inexperience or an honest mistake in oneself, or within one's own group, would be evidence of the inherent inferiority, underperformance, and suspect values of "them".

Then there was the lament from a group of mixed-race heritage: "*First we were not white enough, now we are not black enough!*" In apartheid South Africa, people of mixed-race ancestry classified as "coloured" by the government were allowed some advantages of being closer to whiteness, but suffered many of the disadvantages of being black. Now, a certain group of employees felt that they had been overlooked on account of their identity as coloured, side-lined in favour of black African staff. There was a tendency in this group to identify with "wounded whites" – a realignment of old apartheid affinities (Steyn, 2001).

Phumla believed that resolving the conflict between her and Jeanette was impossible because of the sixth recurring theme: "*Don't mention the R-word!*" In common with many organisations, AMSA had a zero-tolerance policy on discrimination in the workplace. Such policies are intended to be a good thing. The inadvertent result, however, was to force underground hurts, resentments, and limiting assumptions about "the other". There was a deep reluctance to refer openly to race or perceptions of racism – a reticence that included a surprising number of black staff. In group discussions, whites stumbled apologetically over the word "black", and often used the prefix "so-called" with embarrassment when referring to coloured staff. Language once taken for granted under apartheid was now problematised as (mainly) white staff struggled to cleanse their vocabulary of negative imputations. On the other hand, black staff were often blandly cheerful in their assurance that "Everyone gets on here very well", until the safety and confidentiality of one-on-one interviews and small focus group discussions led to disclosures of experiences and perceptions of racism in the workplace. Examples were exclusions from Friday afternoon socialising; lack of access to information; body language demonstrating bored patience or barely contained irritation; covert glances exchanged between certain staff; and conspicuously not being invited with their children to the birthday parties of certain staff members' children, even when part of the same "happy" team.

The continuing story of Phumla and Jeanette

Jeanette had 30 years' experience, was considered a meticulous worker, and had been tasked with mentoring the younger woman when the latter had joined the company some 18 months earlier. Phumla, who had been head-hunted by AMSA for her excellent reputation as an analyst, had been given the impression from the previous manager that she would be inheriting Jeanette's position. Phumla acknowledged that she had learned from her colleague and was grateful for the help, but it was time now to move up as she believed she had a right to expect. She saw her older colleague as adopting an attitude of white superiority, and felt she was being treated as incapable and not being empowered to do her job as she would have liked. Her assumption was that the new head of the team, Belinda, also white, was partisan – on Jeanette's side – because she had not endorsed Phumla's right to inherit Jeanette's position.

Jeanette was deeply alarmed to hear that her colleague expected to have her job – at her age (60), company policy meant that she had no permanent contract;

she had financial needs, and had anticipated renewing her contract at her annual appraisals for at least another three years. She believed Phumla was forcing her out, and could do this because the company espoused a black empowerment strategy. She was also hurt because she thought she had been generous and helpful with knowledge wherever it was needed or asked for. Jeanette felt increasingly angry and silenced. She was shocked to know that Phumla considered her an unmitigated racist.

At the stage when I met them, they had long stopped greeting each other, the air electric with the tension between their desks, separated by only a thin partition. Competing discourses like that of Phumla and Jeanette, especially those operating covertly, hold and incubate divisive and explosive potential. The purpose of the cultural transformation intervention at AMSA was to achieve a sense of alliance towards a shared outcome, an outcome ideally to be shared by diverse individuals and teams.

The four quadrants and validity claims

Wilber (2001b: xiv) does not believe

> that any human mind is capable of 100 per cent error. So instead of asking which approach is right and which is wrong, we assume each approach is true but partial, and then try to figure out how to fit these partial truths together, how to integrate them – not how to pick one and get rid of the others.

Integral mapping offers a platform to interpret an individual's narrative from the positive perspective that the speaker is being *truthful* and unaware that their view is partial – they do not see all the elements available. Wilber (2001b: 12–16; 2001a: 96–109) maintains that each of the four quadrants has its own particular type of truth or validity claim (see Figure 4.1):

- The upper-left quadrant describes the interior state of an individual – the way they feel, what they believe, their *subjective truthfulness*.
- The claim to the validity or proof of the client's narrative is *objectively manifest to the client* – behaviours, management style, performance, body language: the *truth* positioned in the upper-right quadrant. Wilber offers a simple example: in my *truthfulness*, I can say I believe it is raining; the *truth* of this claim is satisfied by looking out of the window – ah, it is indeed raining, an *objective, observable reality*. Phumla and Jeanette, in recounting their version of events, their feelings and assumptions, each believed they were being *truthful*. Moreover, both could provide *evidence* – objective observable reality – the *truth* – that manifestly supported the individual version of each.
- The lower-left quadrant links the subjective world of the individual with the inter-subjective world of relationships – inter-relational values, assumptions, cultural fit, and expectations – including all that we, as a group, believe is *just*.

	Interior	Exterior
Individual	**My truthfulness** based on my values, thoughts, beliefs, hopes, etc.	**Truth** – evidence: manifest behaviour, dress, body language, management style, etc.
Collective	**Justness** – our cultural values, beliefs, aspirations, relationships.	**Functional fit** – appropriate systems, processes, rituals, practices, measurable outcomes.

Figure 4.1 Truthfulness, truth, justness, and functional fit: validity claims. Source: Adapted from Wilber (2001a: 97).

In an ideal world, all members within an organisational culture should share the same inter-subjective space – mutual cultural norms and values, morals, and ethics. If I truthfully hold stealing to be wrong in my subjective world of values, I am happy to subscribe to the *justness* of a community whose values also hold that stealing is wrong. The significance for the individual in the inter-subjective space is the crucial validation of one's identity as a member of that group. This lower-left quadrant of *justness* is about collective agreement on *what is right and fair*. The validity claims between individuals and communities or groups are about cultural fit, mutual recognition.

- Suppose I in my truthfulness, and my community in its justness, hold stealing to be wrong. In that case, there has to be a *functional* way of rewarding honesty and punishing theft – a *fitting* manifest consequence (the lower-right quadrant). How different cultures decide upon *functional fit* for the crime of stealing can vary wildly. In Cape Town, South Africa, a community may decide that the culprit needs to be rehabilitated and committed to performing community service to serve justice. A community in Saudi Arabia may decide that appropriate punishment is to cut off the hand of the thief. Both cultures agree that stealing is wrong. In the case of AMSA, the *justness* of the communal intention to be a values-driven, profit-based entity finds *functional fit*, to give one example, in their performance appraisal system, intended to provide appropriate reward or censure for behaviours that impact the strategic outputs and profitability of the system.

Again, in an ideal world, there would be a harmonious synergy in all four quadrants: the individual and communal subjective interiors of *truthfulness* and *justness*, and individual and collective objective exteriors of *truth* and *functional fit*, would align. In mapping the narratives of Phumla and Jeanette, however, the situation is far from ideal. Each has her own version of truthfulness, evidential truth, justness, and functional fit.

How to reframe validity claims

1. Listen to the person's story

This first stage of the process was to hear, separately, stories of both Phumla and Jeanette – life experiences, background, values, beliefs – and to listen independently to their feelings about, and interpretation of, what each perceived was happening to her (upper-left quadrant – subjective *truthfulness*, the *inner* world of the individual).

Truthfulness: subjective Inner 'I':
Phumla: I am ignored; it hurts, I am an excellent worker with proven high standards, and I am willing to learn. I feel humiliated and angry by the lack of respect from Jeanette.
Jeanette: I believe in high standards and integrity. I hate ingratitude and entitlement. I try to honour what I am asked to do. Phumla's hostility makes me feel ill.

2. Ask for the evidence

Ask for its effect on an individual's actions: what they do as a result of what they perceive. This second stage involved accepting what each saw in the other's behaviour as "truth" or evidential (upper-right quadrant – objective and observable truth as it appears to the individual). Also, each was asked to give examples of what she actually *did* about her thoughts and feelings at work, how she showed her distress, and what effect her distress had on her.

Truth: the observable evidence:
Phumla: My work is "corrected" behind my back; Jeanette talks to my clients about their needs before I do; she stands in the way of my career path. I have stopped greeting her, just do my work and go.
Jeanette: I correct Phumla's work to make her look good. I avoid talking to her and just do what is right.

3. What is just?

Ask about the person's perception of *justness*, what the inter-subjective *community values* should be (lower-left quadrant). Each woman described what she experienced and thought about the organisation's culture, how she interacted with fellow staff members, how she experienced their relationship with her.

Justness: cultural beliefs and values:

Phumla: Black people know how to treat one another better than this. We come to work to do a good job, and we believe in *ubuntu* – I am because you are; we affect one another and should help and care for one another. That's how a good business thrives.

Jeanette: We must do the right thing, try to uphold the core values of excellence and customer service.

4. Ask about functional fit

Finally, the role of each woman in the business was explored (lower-right quadrant – inter-objective contexts), together with each person's understanding of the business outputs, systems, and structures, and examples of how effective and efficient she found these to be.

Functional fit: systemic consequences:

Phumla: The work suffers when people are unhappy. Jeanette should be disciplined. Belinda should take responsibility and remove Jeanette for the sake of the team.

Jeanette: What matters is that the work is delivered error-free and on time for the benefit of the business.

Neither had articulated to the other her assumptions (upper-left quadrant), and tension escalated through the behaviours of each woman (upper-right quadrant) as weeks went by under their new manager, Belinda. Being unfamiliar with her new role and the range of tasks in her new team, Belinda appeared ineffective in her leadership, unable to resolve the impact of rising tension. There was a duplication of functions in Phumla's and Jeanette's roles, resulting in their constantly stepping on each other's toes (systemic breakdown – lower-right quadrant), which added fuel to the fire (organisational culture/values breakdown – lower-left quadrant).

With their permission, I took excerpts from the transcripts of each person's narrative. I mapped out these separately to each woman to illustrate the validity of each individual's claim to truthfulness, truth, justness, and functional fit. When Phumla saw Jeanette's version and *vice versa*, after some resistance, they eventually agreed to meet and talk through their differences on condition that there would also be a mediation session with the new head of the section, Belinda.

Co-creating a common purpose using the quadrants

Phumla and Jeanette then met. The conditions were created for mutual safety and willingness to fully disclose their circumstances as each experienced them, and how this had made them feel and act. We physically mapped these on the quadrants on a whiteboard, including the roles and responsibilities of each, making use of the following questions:

Upper-left quadrant – individual subjective being: How do you need to feel to do your job well? What would you need to believe?

Upper-right quadrant – individual objective behaviours: What would you be doing differently? How would this show up in your role and responsibilities?

Lower-left quadrant – collective organisational values: What do we collectively need to value and measure? What agreements can we make?

Lower-right quadrant – collective systemic outcomes: What is the measurable, practical impact on the business? What is each of our contribution to the business objectives?

The aim was to get each person to hear that the other was speaking and acting from her *truthfulness*. An outcome was surprisingly easily reached, once the willingness of all parties to listen to one another's perspective was established. Phumla accepted that one of her assumptions – that she would inherit the older woman's role as soon as she moved to the new section – was based on inaccurate information from Belinda's predecessor. Belinda took responsibility for taking as long as she had to get to grips with her own and her team's roles, a consequence being the deepening sense of injustice Phumla experienced. Jeanette acceded that she needed to refrain from micromanaging her colleague, and that her intention to be helpful was infantilising and disruptive for Phumla. Belinda's acceptance of her role in the debacle enabled a positive shift for all three individuals in their subjective and inter-subjective spaces, allowing each to reframe what was *just* and *truthful* (upper-left quadrant and lower-left quadrant). On the objective and the systemic side (upper-right quadrant and lower-right quadrant), Jeanette was to mentor Phumla to take over more and more of her role only when Phumla requested her input. This enabled a shift to a mutually acceptable *functional fit*. A commitment from Belinda, as their manager, was undertaken to review their performance contracts with them.

The value of working visually with the four-quadrant validity claims of *truth*, *truthfulness*, *justness*, and *functional fit* is to help an individual see the impact of true but partial assumptions. The act of each of the three women using the quadrants to plot their agreements visibly on the whiteboard achieved several objectives:

1. It enabled each to feel respected and properly heard in their *truthfulness*.
2. This led to each being willing to reframe their perception of the "evidence" – the *truth*.

3. Then they were ready to co-create a shared understanding of *just* and fair shared agreements.
4. Then they were able to design a better *functional fit* for going forward.

The next big step

The interactions between Belinda, Jeanette, and Phumla were symptomatic of a pervasive issue permeating the organisational culture at AMSA, which manifested as a low-trust environment with a consequent impact on performance. There were broken connections between senior management and the development of their managers, and by those managers in the support and development of their staff. There was an overwhelming emphasis on outputs (lower-right quadrant), with little attention to congruence with the espoused organisational culture (lower-left quadrant) and with individual beliefs and manifest behaviours (upper-left quadrant and upper-right quadrant). As issues surfaced through the individual coaching sessions and were then shared in groups, the managing director recognised the need to engage at every level, by creating a shared understanding of what an enabling culture meant and then inviting *co-created* performance measurements and indicators of requisite behavioural competencies.

Chapter 5 describes a group process for creating a shared understanding of an enabling culture. A method was introduced that transformed the way meetings took place and that set the terms for the non-negotiable behaviours which supported increased positivity in a genuinely enabling culture.

Chapter 5

Leading the dance of inclusivity

Leaders and identity construction

Is it possible for a leader-as-coach to lead or coach people in diverse cultural environments without first having insight into the sociological construction of their own identity? There is little research in the coaching and leadership fields into the importance of *self-work* in identity construction or identity transition (Butcher, 2012: 119; Bennett, 2017: 89). There is plenty of research on leadership as a constructed identity, but few articles in journals on the value of leaders understanding *their own identity construction*.

Why does this matter? Understanding oneself as having been shaped by historical, social, cultural, and family influences that differ from group to group enhances the chances of relating well to diverse individuals. The success of relationships is pivotal to a successful organisational climate. All environments are diverse, composed of multiple identities – even those that try not to be. Self-insight into the sociocultural, historical, political, professional, and personal identity construction of the leader is a significant factor, especially when considering the overall culture of an organisation.

The next step at AMSA – from the top to the next layer down

Three months after the initial breakaway with the five ExCo members at AMSA, we came together again to reflect on the impact of the one-on-one coaching. The feedback on some improved team interactions was notable. The overwhelming conclusion of the five ExCo members was the need to involve their direct reports in the insights and skills they were gaining from their individual coaching sessions. It was decided that under the umbrella of their cultural transformation project, ExCo members and their direct reports would gather offsite for a two-day workshop. The objectives were to enable everyone participating to raise controversial issues in a safe environment, and to make joint decisions on the most positive way forward in achieving the sought-after organisational cultural change.

As mentioned in Chapter 1, the results of an internal culture survey made depressing reading – lack of trust, perceptions of racism and discrimination by

DOI: 10.4324/9781003377221-6

all groups, and perceptions of unfairness and inconsistency on the part of senior management. The feedback reflected competing and divisive factions, each with its own recurring narrative or *discursive terrain* – Chapter 4 identified six themes that demonstrated the different impact of historical, socio-political experiences on the identity construction of each faction in a post-apartheid South African setting.

AMSA struggled with diversity issues across several dimensions – positional power, race, gender, status, education, language, religion, and intercultural conflict. The five ExCo members alone represented a world of diversity (apart from all being male and South African): an urbane, agnostic English-speaking white; a deeply conservative Afrikaner Christian; a Jewish systems analyst; a black African Christian; and an Indian Muslim. All except the English-speaker were actively involved in some level of religious and community service. Further, and controversially (both internally and to external stakeholders), the MD had committed the company to non-negotiable black empowerment at every job level. The conservative Afrikaner, loyal and meticulously conscientious, nevertheless criticised the black empowerment project in the company as spurious, arbitrary, and poor business judgement. The outcomes-driven Indian Muslim was irritated with the methodical and cautious Jewish systems analyst; privately, they each pronounced the other's perceived deficiencies as "typical of that type". The black African Christian showed finely tuned awareness of ongoing racial and cultural tensions. Influenced by the company's zero-tolerance policy on discrimination, however, these perceptions were repressed. Each of these five leaders showed *implicit and explicit bias* about one another and their employees.

What is bias?

Neuroscience reveals the vast world of difference in the brain between *learning* (an upper-right quadrant function) and *awareness* (an upper-left quadrant function) (Lewis, Amini, and Lannon, 2001: 107). The former gives rise to *explicit memory* – data we gather from external sources. *Implicit memory* is the storehouse of our awareness – the *interpretation* of our experiences and our emotional reactions to external events (McGilchrist, 2010; Rock and Schwartz, 2006; Rock, 2009). Implicit memory explains the way we interpret a current experience based on an earlier emotional reaction – leaping to a conclusion or making an *assumption*, which may or may not be valid as an interpretation of the current experience. The early messages we receive in life about who we are, what we identify with, and the impact of our experiences seem to be inscribed in our implicit memory. That is, they inform our subjective awareness, with consequences for how we see ourselves and, therefore, how we choose to act in the world.

Regarding interpreting our experiences, when we give our attention to an act or a person or a group, Iain McGilchrist (2010: location 844) observes that "the nature of the attention one brings to bear on anything alters what one finds" and, moreover, that the quality of our attention is influenced by the context. The significance of McGilchrist's observation cannot be overestimated in considering the impact of corporate culture, the "rules of the game", on employees.

From the moment we're born, our brains are busy processing every experience we have – who we see and what we observe happening around us, what we feel, what we do. Our brains begin to make predictions based on these ongoing experiences streaming in. The brain's assimilation of previous experiences works together with the constant activity of *predicting* what we should do, think, or feel from moment to moment (Feldman Barrett, 2017: 58–60). This is how each of us makes sense of our world; previous experiences plus prediction form the basis, an algorithm as it were, for making assumptions – and then making decisions based on those assumptions. Why do some people treat others so badly when confronted with difference? A large part of the answer lies in the impact of early experiences plus prediction, and our innate response to the need to survive. Feldman Barrett (2017: 62) tells us that "Prediction errors aren't problems. They're a normal part of the operating instructions of your brain as it takes in sensory input" (see also Feldman Barrett, 2020; Sapolsky, 2017).

Whether the reaction is to a different race, ethnic group, sexual orientation, or personality style, research on human brain activity indicates that from birth, a combination of nature and nurture predisposes us to discriminate against difference – that which is different from "us". And reversing bias is not so easy:

> While raising awareness can help people to realise that they might be biased, it does not enable them to recognise bias in their own thinking – we simply do not have conscious access to the operations of bias in the brain.
>
> (Lieberman, Rock, Grant Halvorson, and Cox, 2015: 3)

If, from babyhood, you are raised as a Catholic, surrounded by family, friends, and community leaders who are Catholic, and all of whom practise Catholic rituals publicly at church and privately at home, your brain's assimilation of these experiences and its addiction to prediction will probably lead you to assume that religious beliefs and practices other than Catholic are somewhat suspect, or at least not as authentic as yours. You would have an implicit bias in favour of Catholicism and against non-Catholics. Yet, perhaps one day, as a teenager or young adult, you begin to encounter a variety of religious beliefs and practices which lead you to question your certainty about your faith as the only right way.

A coaching colleague recently shared his experience of being born and raised as an evangelical Protestant in the Bible Belt in Texas, where he still lived, having been married to a devout Christian from the same district for nearly 20 years. About ten years previously, he said, he had begun to have an interest in other forms of faith, and came to the conclusion that it should not be sinful to honour the goodness of faiths other than his own, including Buddhism. At first, and for some time, he tried to share with his family and his community his findings, and was distressed by their shocked reactions and their refusals to even hear his experiences – in fact, he became a pariah in his community. His wife remained as devout and committed to her faith and her community as ever, while he built a successful coaching practice which gave him the satisfaction of living his values of supporting others in need – regardless of their faith. What enabled him to overcome implicit and explicit bias is the theme of Chapter 8.

Explicit bias is easier to recognise and deal with than implicit bias. It manifests in cultural rules, practices, and institutions like educational, social, economic, and legal systems. Bias is explicit when social, legal, and political systems enforce, for example:

- that females should not be exposed to formal education, or cannot be permitted to drive, or to play at a particular golf course; or
- that certain groups of people are inferior – as in the case of the lower castes in India, or Jews in Hitler's Germany, or black people under apartheid in South Africa.

We can intervene in explicit bias by changing the overt rules – as in rewriting the national constitution after the demise of apartheid in South Africa in 1994, or outlawing slavery, or granting women the right to vote. We can certainly change the rulebook – but is this enough to change hearts and minds?

Implicit bias is much more difficult to uproot. When explicit bias – like openly using denigrating names to describe members of another group – is named and shamed, implicit bias tends to go underground. According to a headline in a UK tabloid newspaper, the *Daily Mail*, "racism is 'hardwired' into the human brain" (Waugh, 2012) – a dangerously inaccurate interpretation of published academic studies on *bias* and the brain. More truthful is that in under a fifth of a second, our brains react to *difference*, biased either positively or negatively, depending on previous experience and assumptions. We may not consciously recognise that we hold an implicit negative bias against certain groups. The willingness to walk in another's shoes at a deep neurobiological level may depend on whether the person is familiar to us. It appears that strangers do not spark the same level of empathetic response as those who are known to us (Beckes, Coan, and Hasselmo, 2013). A pernicious consequence of negative bias, particularly when it is explicit and legitimised, is the devastating effect on the self-esteem of the denigrated group, an impact often long term and poorly acknowledged.

How does marginalisation happen?

It is useful to recognise the incremental levels from "me" to "we" to "world" to understand oppressive systems and their power to marginalise through explicit and implicit bias. At the individual "me" stage, personal prejudice is not the real danger to social cohesion. The threat is not even in the "we" groups: when individuals band together with those who feel and think as they do. The *real* danger lies in those groups who have the power to set the "rules of the game": the power of leaders of a particular group to determine the rules and to decide what is legal and who is rewarded or punished. When a particular group identity, be it white, male, heterosexual, Christian, Muslim, or Hindu, dominates as the norm and accrues increasing power by maintaining privilege over other group identities for a considerable period, an *ideology of the superiority* of one group is created. The privileged group enjoys greater access to opportunities, resources, and services – and very often, as a result, they gain in self-esteem. For example, an ideology of male superiority has generally prevailed as the result of the three thousand-odd years of power and privilege that has accrued to males across the world through greater access than women to opportunities, resources, and services. Similarly, an ideology of white superiority for at least 500 years in the West has marginalised people of different skin colour.

Taking gender as an example, men, as a historically privileged group in terms of access to opportunities, resources, and services, may very often be blind to the impact of unequal access for women – not because they are deliberately unkind, but because, in the deep, centuries-long embrace of male privilege, they simply cannot see, feel, or relate to what has been experienced by women. For example, a gender-diversity survey of the attitudes and experiences of eBay's top 1,700 global leaders in 2013 found that:

> men and women experience the company in strikingly different ways. A majority of women, for instance, felt that their male colleagues didn't understand them very well, though a majority of men felt well understood by the women. Likewise, women were significantly less likely than men to believe that their opinions were listened to and more likely to doubt that the most deserving people received promotions.
>
> (Angier and Axelrod, 2014: 1–2)

In South Africa, a complaint frequently heard from members of the white population is that, surely, nearly 30 years since the political transition from apartheid in 1994, black people should stop raising issues of white privilege and its negative impact on black people. Indeed, in the USA, more than 200 years since the ratification of the Bill of Rights in 1791, many white citizens are critical of African Americans rallying under the cry "black lives matter". Negative bias is a lived current reality for many women and black people. The good news is that negative implicit bias is definitely not "hardwired" as that British newspaper once suggested, and is changeable with new learning and positive experiences (Phelps and Thomas, 2003).

What can be done about it?

The leader's responsibility is to create safety and the willingness to share and disclose among a group of diverse individuals, whose experience of one another might not predispose them to be vulnerable. Nothing is more effective in stopping the

	Interior	Exterior
Individual	**My attitude** • My assumptions. • Stereotypes. • Prejudices. • Values.	**My behaviour** • Management style. • Leadership style. • Body language. • Policy implementation.
Collective	**Organisational culture** • Group assumptions. • Stereotypes. • Prejudices. • Values.	**Organisational practice** • Systems in use. • Cultural visibility. • Economic access. • Codes of conduct. • Legal frameworks. • Means of production.

Figure 5.1 Quadrant perspective on identity, power, and culture. Source: Aiken (2009: 114).

flow of creative, innovative, and risky thinking than the internalised assumption that "What I think doesn't count."

At AMSA, a workshop process adapted to the four quadrants of the Integral framework became a critical aspect of creating awareness of conscious and unconscious bias and the impact these were having on the psyche of the entire organisation (see Figure 5.1 for an outline of the four-quadrant Integral framing of these issues). An important recognition was that individuals' sharing of information about cultural, gender, religious, or racial differences with one another was not enough to heal rifts – not even close. While this kind of information may have satisfied curiosity and cured ignorance ("Oh, that's why you people do these things!"), it was not enough to guarantee *equality of respect*. When the most hurtful, conflict-ridden barrier to equality of respect was named and brought into the open, a space for healing was created. At AMSA, the most hurtful barrier to equal respect was by far and away limiting assumptions about race by all groups, followed by limiting assumptions about gender.

Four increasing levels of bias

A shared sense of humanity is most important to establish as early as possible in this workshop experience: that every human being, no matter their identity or circumstances, is driven to make choices by the deeply embedded will to survive. Neuroscience provides the evidence that in our quest to survive as best we can, emotions – and the neurochemicals and hormones released with them – shape our beliefs and actions, rather than reason or logic. Recommended reading on this growing body of evidence is Bruce Lipton's (2015) *The Biology of Belief* and Feldman Barrett's (2017) *How Emotions Are Made: The Secret Life of the Brain* and (2020) *Seven-and-a-half Lessons About the Brain*.

An exercise was introduced where important choices needed to be made. (I am deeply indebted to the late Margaret Legum who trained me in the workshop process devised by Ashak Ohrie, co-director of OSDC Ltd, focused on community development, equality, and human rights training.) Participants were asked, initially as individuals, to choose 12 of 20 possible candidates to take with them to build a new society on a fertile, uninhabited island. They were then placed in small groups to reach a consensus on the 12 candidates to accompany them. Very little detail was offered about the candidates, yet it was sufficient to generate heated arguments for and against who would be joining them on the island.

This exercise triggers four increasing levels of bias: conjecture, stereotypes, prejudice, and values:

- *Conjecture* is the most accessible level of bias to reframe. Usually, it does not carry a deep emotional charge. For example, it is an easy adjustment to make in realising that the title "Doctor" of someone to whom you may have just been introduced refers not to a medical doctor but to an academic.
- *Stereotypes* can sometimes be adjusted after persuading the believers with a little relevant information. For instance, the stereotype of all motorbike riders as hard-drinking, drug-taking, violent ruffians may well be tempered if we were to meet a group of mild-mannered accountants on their Sunday ride. Because belief in a stereotype is tinged with more emotional charge than mere conjecture, it may take a little more nudging to dismiss – the willingness to engage in a direct experience.
- *Prejudices* are harder still to dismiss or reframe. When we negatively prejudge a person or a situation, the aversion carries a more profound emotional imprint than a stereotype or conjecture. Prejudging implies we are not even willing to risk a particular encounter, having made up our minds beforehand that it would not be a good experience. So, a degree of persuasion is needed to get us to open up to the experience of a person or situation previously judged undesirable.
- *Values* constitute the most challenging level of all in changing an individual's bias. From the moment we are born, we are surrounded by values. Long before we can utter the word "values", let alone understand it, we are living them. They are deeply imprinted into our brains' survival manual through the culture surrounding us and the rules governing behaviours, especially those deciding reward and punishment. Individuals tend to cluster into groups with others who share similar values – no problem with that, except when one group

assumes the power to make rules that govern all groups. The dominant group has the power to reward or punish, and to decide what rights different groups can enjoy from the cradle to the grave. India's caste system is one example of this; apartheid was another example of differentiated access to services, resources, and opportunities.

Power and marginalisation

Our fragile democracies have barely emerged from millennia of human behaviour which has asserted "I win – you lose": might is right. How power is experienced can become deeply internalised by both the empowered and the powerless. For disempowered or marginalised individuals or groups, a prolonged lack of access to opportunities, resources, and services can cause emotional and psychic wounds that erode self-esteem. The MeToo and Black Lives Matter movements have protested against some of the most extreme forms of oppression of women and African Americans in the USA and elsewhere. Their resonance in the Western world, despite the backlash, has highlighted on a global stage the pain and damage experienced by marginalised and disempowered communities in general. The impact of these realisations in this workshop experience at AMSA was to release a shared vulnerability, an acknowledgement of the degree to which the self-esteem of all groups is caught up in the rules of the dominant group and its systems of reward and punishment. The experiential aspect enabled the participants to recognise what every employee in the building needed – in order to recreate the culture of the organisation, everyone needed to come together with an agreement on shared values and the actionable expression of those values. The workshop experience paved the way for the co-created agreements, developed by the whole AMSA community eventually, of the non-negotiable behaviours all staff members could expect from one another, at any level, in performing their roles.

A word of caution: there is a limit to the long-term success of this workshop process. Powerful as it has proved to be in its capacity to initiate positive alliances across once-alienated groups, its potential weakness becomes evident when it is offered as a stand-alone intervention. Two or three days, however impactful, are not sufficient for embedded shifts in implicit bias, and its manifestations throughout an organisation, a department, or a team – or in an individual. Through my company ProCorp, established in 1998–2014 to focus on marginalisation in the workplace, this workshop process received widespread positive feedback for over a decade in South Africa from individual participants in large private and public organisations, acknowledging its powerful impact. Yet, in the main, it fell short of achieving the most important outcome – positive *organisational culture change* supported by leadership at every level, starting from the top. Nick Petric (2013: 4) comments that:

> We see the same pattern repeat itself with smart, ambitious managers who go to leadership development programmes. The managers gather in a room, and

a trainer teaches them new tools, techniques, and models for how to become a more effective leader. At the end of the programme, everyone commits to making big changes back at work. The managers then return to the job and fall into the same old habits they had before the programme. What's going on?

The road to co-created agreements

What follows is a description of the stages in this process and how they are implemented.

Phase One: The "I" perspective

A critical starting point is to enable the willing participation of everyone involved in the workshop process by dismantling resistance, fear of judgment, fear of being wounded. This is achieved in two steps, the first by asking the team or group of employees what agreements would need to be in place for open, honest, challenging discussions. It matters hugely that people co-create their own conditions for safe participation, rather than the leader expounding a list of company values. The second step to dismantle resistance is the introduction of a light-hearted exercise like the game of choosing 12 out of 20 people to take with you to create a new society on an uninhabited island. This emphasises our shared "humanness": that each individual in the room has knee-jerk opinions, that each of us frequently forms judgments based on very little accurate information – in other words, we display bias: each of us holds conjectures, stereotypes, prejudice, and values.

Phase Two: "I" becomes "we"

Individuals cluster in groups. We form religious groups, music and reading clubs, sports affiliations, business associations, sewing and cooking circles, political groups, and so on. It is central to our survival and sense of wellbeing that we socialise and connect with others "like us". These affiliated groups, like individuals, can display positive or negative values and behaviours: some football clubs have earned negative publicity for racially motivated attacks on players, especially those in opposing teams, for example. Such negative behaviour on the part of one group of individuals towards another is unfortunate, but neuroscience shows us that discrimination is a pattern of survival, an aspect of human behaviour we can expect. When we can all acknowledge as individuals that we are forever assessing, rating, and judging others, positively or negatively, we are ready for the next stage.

Phase Three: The impact of formalised power and privilege of one group on all groups

Negative behaviour of one group towards another becomes extremely damaging when that *one* group holds the power to decide the rules of engagement, reward and punishment, and participation or exclusion. The advantages for the dominant group are enhanced by increased access to opportunities, services, and resources; for example, the continuing disparity of income between men and women of similar status and education within Western organisations.

An ideology of superiority seems easy to inculcate and difficult to overcome for both dominant and marginalised groups, a state of affairs brilliantly illustrated by Jane Elliott, an American schoolteacher, who devised an experience of discrimination for her 8-year-old and 9-year-old white third grade school children after the assassination of Martin Luther King in 1968. The full film of the initiative, *A Class Divided*, and a shorter version, *A Class Divided – Brown Eyes, Blue Eyes Experiment*, are available on YouTube.

As teacher, Jane Elliott had the status and power to make the rules of the game in her classroom: *eye colour* determined the superiority of one group over the other. On the first day of the game, blue-eyed children were deemed superior, told not to play with brown-eyed children, and were given certain privileges not available to brown-eyed children (like being able to go back for second helpings at mealtimes). Members of the "inferior" group were made to wear distinctive collars so that everyone could see at a distance what colour their eyes were. The impact on performance in both groups was remarkable. At the midmorning break on the first day, despite the class having been a warm, cohesive group prior to the start of the game, the blue-eyed children were relishing their "superiority", while the children wearing collars were showing signs of distress, depression, and worst of all, an internalised sense of shame. One boy physically attacked a blue-eyed classmate who taunted him by calling him "brown eyes".

The next morning, Jane Elliott reversed the groups – the brown-eyed children were now on top, and the blue-eyed children lost their privileges and put on the collars. An extraordinary outcome was noted when the disempowered group was reinstated: their performance on a particular word recognition test exceeded anything they had achieved prior to the class experiment. The value of Jane Elliott's experiment is the speed in which it demonstrates the elevated self-esteem of the "superior" group, the internalised low self-esteem of the "inferior" group, and the concomitant impact on performance based on the association of *an arbitrary indicator*: in this case, eye colour. This impact of positive self-esteem on learning skills has been variously researched and affirmed – one need only search the internet on the link between self-esteem and learning ability for children and adults. What matters is how the group holding power and privilege makes the rules that determine the access and participation of all.

Phase Four: Using the quadrants to rethink values and behaviours

This process is devoted to the participants' redesigning inclusivity with an emphasis on diversity. Each individual is encouraged to draw the quadrants on a flipchart and complete their own *upper-left quadrant* by setting out personal values and beliefs in committing to inclusivity.

Their *upper-right quadrant* is populated with individual actions in support of the values and beliefs.

Then the individuals of each small working group get together to design in the *lower-left quadrant* the group's values and behaviours. "The influence of this domain," says Lloyd Chapman (2010: 22), "is very powerful, more so than most individuals would like to admit. South Africa and the issue of affirmative action is a prime example of the power of this domain." In small groups, the participants are invited to notice whether a particular group identity is dominant as the norm in the team, or department, or organisation. These are the kinds of question posed to stimulate bold thinking:

- How has conflict usually been managed? Who speaks up? Who stays silent? So what needs to change?
- Who usually socialises together? Who have been considered outsiders? So what needs to change?
- Who are the dominant talkers at meetings? What group/s often get/s interrupted? So what needs to change?
- Who routinely assumes responsibility for organising the office party or celebratory events? How does this happen, and what needs to change?

The *lower-right quadrant* records the positive performance and business outputs to be expected as a result of the participants' redesign of inclusivity.

At AMSA, this initial two-day workshop was revisited six weeks later, to review its impact on the participants. Positive feedback resulted in the decision that all members in each of the four divisions should experience the workshop and, thereafter, that all groups should commit to revisiting their values and behaviours on a regular basis to reinforce inclusivity and should try to limit the experience of marginalisation from whatever source.

A further development was that the team leaders and the ExCo heads of each of the four divisions committed to adopting a proposal from the teams to improve communications and relationships across all groups: that the teams elect a Management Committee (ManCo). The ManCo members elected from each of the four teams would rotate every quarter, and would be invited to attend and report into the quarterly ExCo meetings. Employees in the four teams generally agreed that there was a breakdown in communication among "tops, middles, and bottoms", to borrow from Barry Oshry's (2007) terminology: information or instructions were pushed down the line from ExCo, but very little opinion or observations from the staff seemed to be welcomed by ExCo. This top–down dynamic was described as an outdated display of positional power and privilege, the impact of which stifled innovation and participation in so-called solutions-focused discussions.

Chapter 6 describes critical capacities that enabled these teams to communicate with one another and to build on the best ideas – the ability to hold effective meetings.

Chapter 6

Leading a listening culture

The key to raising the EQ of individuals and groups – managing meetings

Chapter 1 introduced a senior group of executives who were committed to the transformation of the culture of their organisation from a climate of hostility and cynicism to one of positive engagement. At the breakaway to plan the first six months, there was a critical practice which the leadership team needed to experience and learn to embody before they would be able to agree on the way forward, let alone action their plan – the ability to listen, truly listen, to one another. They needed to get out of the way of each other's thinking by suspending judgment, and by giving one another uninterrupted attention.

When I ask managers and team members what they find most frustrating about their work, the answer, almost always, is *meetings!* The list of complaints is almost identical across a range of organisations, and interestingly, the intensity of the frustration of employees seems to increase with the attendance of senior managers. Here is a typical litany of complaints – see which ones resonate with you:

- Meetings are too frequent.
- There is no agenda.
- People arrive late.
- The agenda is not adhered to.
- People come ill prepared.
- People are focused more on their mobile phones and tablets than on the purpose of the meeting.
- The same people dominate.
- People interrupt.
- Meetings are too long.
- We keep revisiting the same issues.
- Boring! Why am I there at all?

Meetings are an essential part of organisational life, but from the widespread complaints, it seems they are all too frequently inefficient in managing time, sharing

DOI: 10.4324/9781003377221-7

accurate information, and achieving outcomes. However, acclaimed authors and practitioners like Nancy Kline (1999, 2009, 2020), Bill Torbert (2004), Robert Kegan and Lisa Lahey (2001), Bill Robertson (2015), David Rock in an interview with Jeremy Schwartz (Rock and Schwartz, 2006), and Amy Edmondson (2019) promise us it doesn't have to be this way. Each emphasises a particular ability as a critical leadership competency – the art of *listening*.

The process for creating a listening culture is a daring practice to lead, at first. It asks leaders to step back from command and control, to let go of the need to be the expert, and to trust others to think for themselves, to trust in the very intelligence for which staff were employed. In meeting this way, the leader or chair assumes that their team could probably have good ideas or even better ones than they could have. In such a meeting, the leader or chair regards giving the team their point of view as a last resort – not as a first step.

The transformative power of a listening culture

Kevin Sharer, then CEO and Chairperson of Amgen, a multinational biopharmaceutical company headquartered in California, recounts in a 2012 interview with McKinsey & Company his discovery of the importance of listening to understand what the other person was trying to convey:

> as you become a senior leader, it's a lot less about convincing people and more about benefitting from complex information and getting the best out of the people you work with. Listening for comprehension helps you get that information, of course, but it's more than that: it's also the greatest sign of respect you can give someone.
>
> (Sharer, 2012: 1)

He emphasises the importance of "strategic listening" to enable senior executives to get the information vital for successful leadership of their companies from their "ecosystems" – including their direct reports, other staff members within their organisations, the media, surveys and reports, industry analysts, and external stakeholders such as shareholders:

> organisations that don't listen will fail, because they won't sense a changing environment or requirements or know whether their customers or employees are happy. In an incredibly information-intensive, dynamic environment, you have to listen or else – to mix metaphors – you're blind.
>
> (Sharer, 2012: 2)

Nancy Kline focuses on the importance of listening in creating the optimum environment for all people (whether employers, stakeholders, or clients) to think freshly, boldly, and freely. She maintains that a high quality of attention while listening is so palpable that it ignites the ability of individuals to think well in its presence. Neuroscience confirms Nancy Kline's assertion that such attention is a catalyst: "a substance that increases the rate of change without being consumed or changed itself" (Kline, 2009: 35). The core principle of the power of attention and the importance of listening is emphasised in each of her books (Kline, 1999, 2009, 2020).

Irrespective of differing worldviews and degrees of cognitive complexity, the practice of listening without interruption encourages listeners to put a hold on a knee-jerk reaction in favour of a more considered response. It is in fact the magic, the *open-sesame*, to engaging an entire team or organisation in the aspirations of a transformed world of work. There are several skilful methodologies which honour these principles. I am grateful to have been taught by Nancy Kline as coach, consultant, and facilitator of the Thinking Environment® (2004–2005), as well as being a foundational member of the Time to Think Collegiate. The case studies provided here illustrate the Time to Think philosophy and practices advocated by Nancy Kline.

The power of listening with positive regard

The primary motivation for truly listening is interest in people and what they think. More than one manager has asked, "How can you listen with rapt attention if someone is talking rubbish?" Kline's (2005) advice is that even if it seems to be "rubbish" to you, the steadfastness of your listening allows a person to become more authentic in your presence. It matters what people say, but it matters even more what happens for them because they say it. In the process of exploring their own thinking, the listener's comments on the person's thoughts are not particularly useful and might even be derailing. According to Kegan and Lahey (2001: 14), "The ground rule in your role as a listener is this: it is not your job to point out to someone something you think he or she may be missing." A person will continue the process of thinking for as long as they have this quality of attention. The addiction to helping, to being directive as a leader or a coach, is more easily overcome with deep self-awareness of one's quality of attention – it is a great skill.

The positive philosophical choice embodied in listening this way, according to Kline, is a preference for the assumption that most human beings are born essentially good, worthy of receiving respect. It embraces Kant's categorical imperative, his Golden Rule that we should behave towards others as we expect to be treated. In alignment with the Rogerian principle of (most) human beings as inherently good, it offers the structured practice of being able to recognise the value of self and the value of others, and to actively treat one another from this perspective.

Sometimes senior leaders have shaken their heads in disbelief at what they perceive to be a hopelessly idealistic approach to human nature, and one that they assume dodges the hard conversations. Yet this approach is probably the toughest discipline we can master in the interest of delivering high-trust, high-performance results. The wisdom lies in the thinking of the full group, including the leader. Everyone in these meetings is equal as a thinker, regardless of positional power.

In order to access the wisdom of the group, clear guidelines need to be in place. To adopt an unconditionally positive regard for each individual one encounters is not an easy path to tread! It is frequently difficult to absorb positive regard for ourselves, let alone others.

Indeed, evidence-based research from, for example, Israel (2020) and Jeremiah (2016), is giving us the metrics that show the remarkably consistent degree of success in outputs when the conditions for positive engagement are present. These conditions are essential in enabling the *psychological safety* that facilitates having tough conversations and giving difficult feedback. Psychological safety, named by Amy Edmondson (2019), prompted researchers to recognise its critical role in what constitutes high performance in teams at Google: quite simply the conditions that were found to create psychological safety were "conversational turn-taking and empathy" – the lack of which is a sad indictment of organisational life. This important research on Google by Duhigg (2016: 5) found that "As long as everyone got a chance to talk, the team did well. But if only one person or a small group spoke all the time, the collective intelligence declined." Providing the conditions that enable courageous new thinking in the presence of others is perhaps the single most important leadership attribute in meeting the challenges of the twenty-first century.

Managing a Thinking Environment meeting

The optimum benefit of running meetings as a Thinking Environment is the generation of fresh creative thinking: planning the future, solving a problem, seeking innovation. Critical to managing these meetings successfully is the skill of the chairperson, or the leader of the meeting. It is just as important, however, for each participant to experience and buy into the concept of managing meetings this way. Shifting from low trust to high trust requires consistency of critical behaviours across multiple job levels and functions – hence the value of training key individuals, team leaders, and groups throughout the organisation with this values-based, systematic approach. It is always advisable to seek training from someone certified in these practices before attempting to instil them in an organisation or team.

The agenda: Asking the right questions

The first key difference in chairing meetings this way is that the agenda is drawn up in the form of *questions*. The brain thinks in a more focused and efficient way in the presence of a clear question than in response to a header. Rather than the usual categories of "Customer Service", "Financials", "Other", and so on, the leader of the meeting clearly poses the question that most needs to be addressed in each category on the agenda. Under "Financials", for example, the most pressing question might be "How can we address the outstanding payments due to us?" This requires the leader of the meeting – and those attending – to take time to prepare in order to formulate as a question the most pressing issues needing to be addressed.

Opening the meeting

An important first step is to establish an environment of positive engagement. The aim of the *first question* that opens a meeting is to raise the quality of attention in the room, to get every participant to listen to one another with curiosity and interest. So the question might be something like: "What is going well for you at the moment?" or "What's one thing that has pleased you at work this week?"

The first question in a brief opening round of this first meeting at AMSA was:

> What is an attribute or quality you demonstrate in your current position of which you are most proud?

This question asked for a degree of vulnerability in venturing disclosure: having already established a relationship with the members, it was worth risking. Its purpose was to bring the attention of the group into tight focus, to get them interested in knowing their colleagues more deeply, and to have each individual appreciate and build positively on what they held to be good and true. A further purpose was to shift focus from beginning with a negative and retrospective re-iteration of the problems to starting with what is working well and worth building on.

Rounds

Rounds are a valuable enabling part of the process in these meetings. The leader asks that whoever wishes to speak first indicates, when they have had their say, whether the next speaker is to continue to their right or to their left. This ensures that each person has their time to talk and knows when their turn is coming. Unlike a "popcorn" approach, which can be nerve-wracking for the less confident, a round enables the reticent personalities – and those responding in their second or third language – to participate as fully as the more outgoing, confident individuals.

No one is interrupted

For each member present at a meeting to give this quality of attention means that *no speaker will be interrupted*. Kline (2022, pers. com.) points out, "The promise of no interruption and of generative attention include interest in where the person will go *next* with their thinking ... the steadfastness of your listening allows a person to become more authentic and intelligent in your presence." Holding this fundamental discipline has often been quite a challenge for participants. In itself, the commitment to listening without interruption requires that individuals be constantly aware of their own internal chatter, of resisting the desire to butt in. The long-term effect of this practice is to raise the emotional intelligence of the group, as learning impulse control and resisting the desire to interrupt becomes embedded. The reward is increased efficiency and effectiveness in achieving positive outcomes.

Input is time-bound

The skill of leading a meeting with no interruptions requires clear parameters. Each member needs to know categorically that their thinking is welcome and will be heard – and in order for this to happen within the allocated meeting schedule, the leader clearly establishes upfront *the amount of time* that each person can have to make their contribution. Each participant knows that they can expect equality of participation and equality of time and that their contribution will be treated with equality as a valued thinker, regardless of position or status. It also means that each thinker has the obligation:

- to compose their thoughts efficiently in the time allotted;
- to focus specifically on the question that has been framed; and
- to build positively on the thinking of others without repeating what has already been said.

These conditions ensure that there is freedom from negative competitiveness, in the interest of co-creating the best idea.

The second question in a round with the ExCo at AMSA, and the core point of this meeting, was:

What would each of you want to see as the most positive outcome of this intervention for the company?

Thinking pairs

Making use of the process step of *thinking pairs*, we split into pairs with the instruction that each member of a pair had their own three minutes to think out loud about the question. The partner is asked to listen for the full three minutes with no interruption, asking no leading questions, making no comment. The role of the partner is to listen with such fine yet non-intrusive attention that it inspires free-ranging and creative thinking in their colleague. Then after three minutes, the role of listener/thinker is reversed. When experiencing this process for the first time, at the completion of each pair's "think" (six minutes in total, in this example), it is advisable for the chair or leader who debriefs the process to ask each person what it was like as the thinker to have three minutes to think out loud without interruption, and to ask how each person experienced being the listener.

Some people are natural born listeners, gifted with that quality of attention that enables the thinker to immerse themselves fully in their topic. Many, however, claim that they find it really difficult not to interrupt, not to ask questions or give advice. Apart from being socialised to interact when someone speaks to us, our curiosity and need to know push us to intervene, to ask for clarity, context, and so on. The process of thinking pairs asks that the listener be entirely in the service of the thinker – such questions are only for the benefit of the listener, and might well obstruct the thinker's ability to explore their topic. In a thinking pair, the listener has no need to be a subject expert on the thinker's topic: the dynamic quality of the listener's attention and interest alone is the equivalent of a magnetic force-field, attracting the partner's rising thoughts. On the thinker's side, most people report that not being interrupted, second-guessed, or questioned is sheer heaven. Others say it feels very awkward not to have verbal interaction with their partner – even embarrassing. It takes some discipline, and certainly iterations of practice, to fully appreciate the generative benefits of this time-efficient process.

Noting the outcomes

Next, each person in a round is asked for *one* important outcome of their three-minute think – to be given *in one short sentence*, if possible. The effect of this request is to focus the mind on the most salient issue, efficiently expressed, avoiding long, rambling, and time-consuming explanations. This input is important to capture (on a flipchart or screen) in the speaker's own words. The round continues until each member has put up all of their thinking. An advantage of asking for just one point at a time from each person is the opportunity to appreciate group-think – very often participants find that a colleague has come up with exactly their thought. If just one participant sets out all their points in one go, it might well pre-empt others from participating, and the appreciation of experiencing colleagues "on the same page" would be lost. This was especially important to establish in this meeting with AMSA where two members of the Executive Committee were in conflict, one of them holding negative assumptions regarding his colleague's ability to think creatively and intelligently about cross-functional solutions in their joint projects.

We then considered the "wish list" on the flipchart of the most positive outcomes of this intervention for the company. Recording each person's statements or ideas visually on a flipchart or whiteboard demonstrated the underpinning positive philosophy of the Thinking Environment – each person's thinking matters, each contribution counts. It enabled the group to build co-operatively on the best idea, rather than competing with one another.

What are we assuming?

One of the most powerful questions I have ever been asked, which came up in training with Nancy Kline and which I have used with clients frequently since, was: "What do you assume most of the time that limits your happiness?" It can be life changing to realise that that particular limiting belief is standing in the way of achieving one's potential, especially when it is not based on any credible evidence.

Taking each wished-for outcome in turn, the next question was:

What are you assuming that most stands in the way of achieving this goal?

They considered whether the assumption was untrue, true, or possibly true. Each of these three options is considered against all of the following criteria:

- Are we assuming the most positive outcome?
- Is the assumption logical?
- Is it based on evidence or accurate information?

The easiest limiting assumption to dismantle is one that is shown, on evidence, to be untrue. For example, a concern at this ExCo meeting was the compatibility of a newly installed and costly system with existing programmes. The head of Operations and the head of Services each blamed the other for obstruction and scope creep, with the consequences of time and money wasted. When each member of the Executive team tested the assumption (that the new system was incompatible with existing programmes) against evidence, logic, and shared information, they arrived at the positive conclusion that the assumption was untrue. In fact, their teams did indeed have the skills and resources to integrate the two systems successfully.

Given that nothing in the respective teams had changed since the start of this ExCo meeting, why were these two men unable to come to this conclusion before? They were both highly experienced, seasoned in debate, and used to managing conflict in tough, pressurised environments – yet neither had found a way to arrive at the positive outcome they reached at this meeting. The simple answer is that the structure and processes of meeting this way provided the conditions to engage with goodwill, to think aloud about one's assumptions without fear of devastating criticism, without defensiveness. The "rules" enabled the participants to maintain a disciplined regard for one another's ability to think well. They also provided the optimum conditions for contributing to problem-solving.

The participants' thinking was further facilitated by asking an *incisive question*. As a critical component of the Thinking Environment, incisive questions are the most powerful liberating driver of solutions-focused thinking. The Ten Components constituting the conditions for a Thinking Environment are fully explained in Nancy Kline's books (1999, 2009, 2020). The "king" component is attention. Each of the remaining components gains increased value in its presence: equality, ease, appreciation, information, feelings, diversity, encouragement, incisive questions, and place. They cut through clouded, stuck thinking to release clear and positive possibilities. In Nancy Kline's words, an incisive question is one that "replaces an untrue limiting assumption with a true liberating one and connects that assumption to the desired outcome of the person or group" (Kline, 2022, pers. com.). The incisive question was: "If you knew that the compatibility of the new system is indeed possible with the teams you have, what actions will you now take?"

Their answers led to a productive, rapid, open discussion of strategies that were recorded on a flipchart using the four quadrants to map hopes and intentions (upper-left quadrant), action steps that set out how and by whom (upper-right quadrant, lower-left quadrant), and a schedule for monitoring and evaluating impact (lower-right quadrant).

Regarding the two colleagues in conflict in Chapter 4, the component of *information* played a crucial role in reframing their regard for each other. Being able to be heard without interruption gave each the opportunity to explain key aspects and challenges of their and their team's roles and functions. Also, the three other ExCo members were able to add information that they had previously not even known might be useful. The prevailing protocol of non-interference in each other's functions, in spite of the damaging impact of the conflict on their own areas, had kept each silent in their own siloed domain.

To this end, a further question was:

> What do each of you most need from one another to in order to achieve your best outcomes?

The power of positive language

Questions are framed in positive language – the language we use has an enormous impact on the thinking and feeling of others (Kegan and Lahey, 2001). Neuroscientific research on our brain functions makes apparent the physiological consequences and split-second speed of the flight-or-fight reactions of our limbic brain. I could just as easily have asked, "What have you found most unhelpful in working with one another?" The quality of response to *this* question is unlikely to build positive engagement. Similarly, a question such as, "What went wrong with performance last quarter?" could easily slide into blame and recrimination as people dive to defend their roles in a past event. Reframing the question in positive language: "*What could each of us be doing differently to achieve better results this quarter?*" still engages with the hard issues of last quarter's performance, but with a positive, solutions-focused intention.

The penultimate round of this session before closure introduced the practice of *appreciation* – another of the Ten Components of the Thinking Environment that is so often neglected in our daily lives. Nancy Kline maintains that we should strive for a 5:1 ratio of appreciation to criticism. The positive reflection given by each person in the opening round had already enabled participants to experience the uplifting effect of appreciation. The participants were asked to give an appreciation to their colleague (on their left or right) on an aspect they most valued in that person. There were some self-conscious glances and some squirming, but each rose to the task – and with gracious eloquence. The surprised gratitude on the faces of the recipients made the point – relevant and credible affirmations elevate our self-esteem, raise energy levels, and enhance our wellbeing.

Closing the meeting – focus on positive outcomes

The question for the closing round asks of the group:

> What outcomes are you particularly pleased with, from your experience today?

One could also ask, "What are you happy to commit to from this meeting?" A vital aspect of this process is its focus on the achievement of positive outcomes. Part of the intention of this closing round is that participants value, in their own words, all that has been positive and useful to them in the meeting. The very act of uttering these words is important: putting one's thoughts into articulate sentences firms up the reality of what is being said. A further purpose of the closing round is confirmation for the leader that the meeting objectives and outcomes have been well understood by participants, who were positively involved every minute.

Following on

Three months after this ExCo meeting, the five members were unanimous in their desire to escalate this intervention to include their direct reports. The recognition was that problems in communication, especially concerning cross-functional matters, were prolific throughout the company, starting with themselves. They agreed that high-trust, high-performance teams could happen only with robust, open communication up and down the line. Yet they were fearful that bringing issues into the open might deepen the rifts they were anxious to mend. Based on their own experience of the outcomes from their first practice in meeting this way, however, the MD expressed his confidence in the benefits of continuing this style of meeting.

A breakaway venue was chosen, and 18 senior members representing each of the four divisions of the company were to convene there over three days. After introductions, and setting the overall intention of the breakaway, the first round of the session opened with a light, positive question:

What was your best moment at work this week?

As noted above, the purpose was to raise the interest and energy levels in the quality of attention of the participants. In the following round, the participants were asked:

What would make this company an enabling environment for you?

Their answers generally reflected the complaints raised in the internal staff climate survey, but following Thinking Environment principles, the phrasing of the question elicited responses in positive terms – respect, timely communications, non-racialism, understanding of each other's cultures and religions, consistency of remuneration for the same job level, and senior managers who "walk their talk" were some of the responses on the flipcharts. By Day Three, process and components of meeting this way were embedded sufficiently for the MD to take over.

The MD had prepared the key questions that he saw as important for unleashing the most productive outcomes. He was also willing to "dance in the moment" should circumstances demand, recognising the potential limitations of casting his agenda questions "in stone". The information generated by rounds, pairs, team dialogue, and full-group open discussion in the previous two days had not only raised previously unspoken sensitive issues above the waterline in safety and an atmosphere of goodwill; the group had now drawn up on flipcharts a co-created agreement of the *assumptions* that stood in the way of their goal of being in a high-trust, high-performance environment.

A limiting assumption that all agreed was true, based on evidence, was the *lack of timeous and relevant communication* across their four divisions. A further true limiting assumption was that in the current structure, no functional mechanisms were in place to facilitate what would appear to be a complex network of intercommunication. Another assumption was that different mindsets and perspectives in each division, with the staff in each division focused on achieving their specific range of outcomes, tended to obstruct co-operation. The key limiting assumption they came up against was:

> *Our current structure and the necessary different roles of the four divisions work against timely and effective communication that enables the free flow of information.*

The group then broke into pairs to generate the freshest thoughts of each person. The room was electric with the buzz of voices, every person engaged and productive. Pair work, as *thinking pairs* or *dialogue*, has the double benefit of engaging the full group in creative thinking at the same time and of enabling individuals to explore their thinking before being exposed to the whole group, thus overcoming fear of judgment, of "saying something stupid". It ensures that every member is involved and contributing. No one at this meeting was bored to tears, surreptitiously occupied with their mobile phones, wishing they were somewhere else. It also produced, in the most efficient use of time, a burst of ideas that were then harvested in a round and mapped on the quadrants to make sure there were no blind spots, enabling the full group to begin to firm up common suggestions and build on the best ideas.

The co-created outcome was the suggestion, mentioned in Chapter 5, to establish a Management Committee (ManCo). The participants agreed that the conditions for its success depended on the maintenance of meeting this way as intrinsic to the organisational culture, to replace the hierarchical, top–down tradition of communication, and to dismantle silo management. Their proposed plan of action was for ManCo to meet with ExCo once a month to share information *up and down* the line – changing the conventional culture of top–down communication. ManCo would also be responsible for appointing a representative member from each division to maintain cross-functional lines of communication by attending project meetings outside their own mandate. A team of accredited coaches and consultants would be assembled to expose all staff to the processes and principles of meeting this way, as well as training champions in leading such meetings. These steps were accomplished over the six months that followed.

Everyone at this breakaway felt excited by the renewed motivation it had inspired. A triumphant outcome was that participants were united in their view that the issues that stood in the way of trust and motivation (raised on Day One) had been satisfactorily addressed. Further, if their experience of meeting this way became the culture (or climate) of the organisation, most of the issues would be unlikely to resurface in the future. The MD and his ExCo were, however, under no illusions about what it would take to embed this way of meeting throughout the company, and knew that they would need to lead the way. As Goleman, Boyatzis, and McKee (2013: 18) point out: "If climate drives business results, what drives climate? Roughly 50 to 70 per cent of how employees perceive their organisation's climate can be traced to the actions of one person: the leader."

There were several matters that would need to be dealt with – like reviewing the complaints regarding too many unnecessary meetings, with the wrong people attending – to streamline ManCo's functioning.

Selecting champions at every level

The quality of meetings raises a question about the overall design of a transformational organisational culture intervention (Edwards, 2009; Kotter, 2012). The purpose and most powerful impact of a Thinking Environment is the igniting of independent thinking. Its Ten Components allow people to think for themselves. Sustainable transformation of organisational culture to include meeting this way would mean a careful selection of *champions* at every level. The position and power of these champions of change at every level enhances the scope of their circle of influence. Also, it is well worth rethinking the use of one-on-one coaching interventions which cater for (mostly) willing, individual middle or senior managers who often set their own agenda. Instead, consider using team workshops led by those trained in managing meeting skills, in combination with individual coaching focusing on overall leadership development strategy (Anthony, 2017). The joint contribution guarantees the widest dissemination into the company of the relational competencies, processes, and structures that support an emotionally intelligent, high-performance culture.

Chapter 7 describes an approach for individuals and teams to increase self-awareness and self-management, as well as awareness of others and managing relationships with others skilfully.

The Enneagram

Self-awareness and relationship management

The Enneagram

In the drive to create more relational and personal awareness in leaders and managers, organisations commonly use standard 360° feedback processes and typologies like the Myers-Briggs Type Indicator® and Insights®. More frequently these days, they may opt to offer an Enneagram questionnaire to their employees. The Enneagram (which means "nine signs" in Greek) is variously referred to as a basic personality test, a character typing, an invitation to personal development, and a way of understanding similarities and differences within groups.

It is purported to have ancient roots dating back 2,500 years, although this is in doubt, and its origins are unclear. It underwent a revival in the nineteenth century with the flowering of psychology. An emphasis on the message of healing was carried into the twentieth century, notably by the charismatic Chilean-born psychiatrist Claudio Naranjo (1932–2019). Later interpretations, like those of A.H. Almaas (2021), Jerome Wagner (1996), and Susan Rhodes (2013), emphasise positive values rather than our weaknesses, and hence nine healthy characteristics of a person's authentic self. This positive interpretation suggests that over time, and in the interests of self-protection, we tend to become habituated to one or two particular patterns of values and behaviours, especially those for which we are rewarded from early childhood (Wagner, 1996: 6–7).

Neuroscientific validation of the Enneagram

Neuroscience supports the theory that our brains have formed algorithms of values and patterns of behaviour in pre-verbal infancy, patterns that originate in closely observing our carers in a drive to enhance our survival, and these endure into adulthood as our survival strategies. A further validation of the Enneagram by neuroscientific research is its interpretation and integration of three brains: the head, heart, and gut brain. Neuroscience reveals that our head brain, heart brain, and gut brain interconnect in a constant dynamic and complex relationship, disclosing the impact of our thoughts and our emotions on our individual wellbeing and on our immune

DOI: 10.4324/9781003377221-8

system, and also the impact we have on one another (Feldman Barrett, 2020, 2017; Blake, 2018; Siegel, 2017, 2018; Lipton, 2015).

The heart with its estimated 40,000 neurons communicates with the brain in more ways than one: via the vagus nerve, the heart sends more signals to the brain than the brain to the heart. The team that developed HeartMath (founded by Doc Childre in 1991) recognised through these findings that emotions have a physiological reality. It's no accident that someone can say, "I love you with all my heart" rather than "I love you with all my head" – love is a strong emotional, physiological feeling. The heart can sense these feelings, it learns and remembers, sending messages to the brain about how the body is feeling. Even more wonderful is the knowledge that the heart is capable of *neuroplasticity* – the ability of cells to learn and change in response to new input and new practices. Imagine the consequences of this for acquiring healthy resilience.

Our gut brain is "as large and as chemically complex as the grey matter in our heads", says Giulia Enders (2015), author of a fascinating and very frank account of our gut "from end to end". She tells us that more than 90 per cent of serotonin, a hormone and neurochemical which promotes happiness and whose absence is related to depression, is produced in the gut. Serotonin also accounts for feeling deliciously sleepy after a good lunch. When we intuit something, we have "gut feelings"; when we feel nervous anticipation, we feel "butterflies in our tummies"; when our patience with someone has reached the limit, we've had "a gutsful". When something or someone is repulsive to us, we feel "nauseated", "sick to my stomach". These emotional reactions are in part a result of the gut's interaction with a part of the brain called the insula, which receives information about feelings from the entire body (Enders, 2015).

The purpose of pointing out these head–brain, heart–brain, gut–brain connections in the context of the Enneagram is to emphasise that relationship is not just a "mental" thing or a "heart" thing, but an intricate interconnection of head, heart, and gut: "What we do inside relationships matters more than any other aspect of human life" (Lewis, Amini, and Lannon, 2001: 192). Through our human interaction we literally cause change in one another's brains, for better or worse (Feldman Barrett, 2020). Could anything be more significant for the relationship between managers and staff, or coach and client?

The Enneagram positions these three brains as *centres of expression*. Each of these three centres seeks to satisfy a fundamental need: the gut centre seeks *autonomy*, the heart centre seeks *attention*, and the head centre seeks *security*. Each centre embraces three of the nine Enneagram types or patterns (see Figure 7.1), each of which meets its fundamental need in one of three ways – by earning, demanding, or withdrawing to gratify its needs. Ideally, a truly integrated personality would have access to each centre of expression and all nine authentic values and behaviours contained in them, knowing which to draw on in different situations.

Amy Edmondson (2019: location 333) maintains that hiring talented individuals is not enough if they are unable to work well together. Using the Enneagram with individuals and within their teams highlights the importance of both-and, of parts

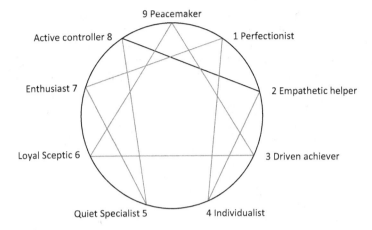

Figure 7.1 The nine types of the Enneagram. Source: Adapted from multiple sources.

and whole – *holons* and *holarchies*, discussed in Chapter 2 (and again in Chapter 8). Just as each quadrant represents its own kind of enquiry, so does each Enneagram style, and each has its particular way of evolving, with the potential for vertical development. As for the individual, so for the team. There is no benefit in a focus solely on the parts, to the detriment of a focus on the whole. Equally, we should not focus on the whole and ignore the parts. As Susan Rhodes (2006: 10) suggests:

> If we think of each human being as a holon – which we are – then we know that each of us has a role to play as an autonomous individual (a whole) and also a participant (a part) in something greater than ourselves.

A great aspect of the Enneagram, positioned by experts like Jerome Wagner (1996, 2010), is an injunction not to judge ourselves with blame for our patterns. Instead of regarding ourselves as "bad" or what we do as "wrong", it is more useful to think about how we have been trying to keep ourselves safe in the best ways we know how – basic survival strategies. Neuroscientific research tells us that these survival strategies are created from birth, and are reinforced by repetitive experiences:

> trapped within the skull, with only past experiences as a guide, your brain makes predictions. Through prediction, your brain constructs the world you experience. It combines bits and pieces of your past and estimates how likely each bit applies in your current situation.
>
> (Feldman Barrett, 2017: 59)

As we grow into adulthood, our survival strategies may need reviewing and adjusting to a range of behaviours and relationships that were not in the spectrum of our awareness when we were children. When we fail to undertake new learning about others and make these adjustments, we might become stuck in a limited version of the world, viewing difference through the lens of judgment and blame. The Enneagram brings awareness of our own deep patterning, our quadrant "sweet spots" and "blind spots" (see Chapter 2). Through inviting self-awareness and reflection, it encourages the acquisition of greater wisdom. Significantly for teams and organisations, it has the potential to increase compassion and understanding for others by recognising the different survival strategies and coping mechanisms of colleagues. Managers and leaders discover the benefits of a more flexible style which considers the opinions and needs of others, rather than an inflexible "I-am-the-expert" approach.

The power of emotions at work

As a business leader or team leader, you want your people to bring the best of their brains to work, to connect positively with one another, to find effective solutions in delivering on projects that are constantly changing. This means building a robust environment for courageous or "crucial" conversations. Patterson, Grenny, McMillan, and Switzler (2002: 1–3) propose that the fundamental cause of many of our problems stems from the way people behave when others disagree with them, especially about emotional issues when there is a lot at stake. What matters is the creation of an environment where everyone, regardless of their status in the organisational hierarchy, feels safe enough to raise contentious issues in the interest of finding the best solutions.

What stops people at work from raising a difficult issue or a controversial perspective? What stops people from being critical or naming a problem – especially in the presence of positional power? Think about what might stop you. Underlying each of our Enneagram patterns is its own fundamental fear – fear of rejection, of being unloved for not being good enough, assertive enough, helpful enough, perfect enough, cautious enough – underlying fears that Nancy Kline might call our *bedrock* self-limiting assumptions (Kline, 1999: 167–174). This fundamental fear causes us to be vulnerable to interpersonal pressure. We don't want to look foolish in front of others; we don't want to hurt someone's feelings; perhaps we are not sure of all the facts; perhaps we do not have the courage "to speak truth to power", because we have seen how aggressively or how negatively our manager – or certain team members – can react.

Working with our Enneagram patterns as individuals and in teams helps us recognise that it is not our cognitive ability that inhibits a courageous conversation; it's our emotional networks that react with a *fight, flight, or freeze* response in under a fifth of a second (Rock, 2008: 2).

Kupers and Weibler (2008: 259) remind us that "emotions are brought into play by the actions of others, and as such, they influence and are influenced by interpersonal relationships and social situations". Yet, they point out that for the longest time the vital role of emotions in the optimum functioning of an organisation has not been considered sufficiently important for research, until recently. Emotions have been considered inappropriate, irrational – the antithesis to logical thinking in organisational life. There is, however, growing recognition that emotions "inform, shape, and reflect the life of organisations in various ways. Importantly, feelings and emotions influence the way members of organisations perceive, interpret, control, and evaluate their own and shared states and actions" (Kupers and Weibler, 2008: 261). Being aware of one's own Enneagram pattern and learning about the range of patterns that exist in our families, in teams, and among our clients is a very positive step on the road to managing relationships not only well but courageously. According to Lisa Feldman Barrett (2017: 242–243), "Emotional harm can shorten your life … emotional harm can do more serious damage, last longer, and cause more future harm than breaking a bone."

Teamwork with the Enneagram

The owner of an architectural design firm expressed interest in experiencing the potential of the Enneagram profile to enhance the interactions of a top team of architects and designers who also had a role in troubleshooting, maintaining efficiency, and solving crises that arose in some of the many projects they ran. The overall purposes were to improve their interaction with one another, and to improve their leadership skills in working with problems that arose with teams in other areas of the business. According to the owner, his personal experience of the nine styles of the Enneagram spectrum had given him insight into an interpretation of his own patterns and those of others that left him feeling freer, less judgmental, and more empowered in raising difficult or controversial issues. As the leader of this top team of architects and designers, his strong wish was to remove some of the inhibitors and limitations in his team's interactions, particularly the reluctance to speak frankly when controversial issues arose. There was a certain uneasiness as each member of the team agreed to have their own personal Enneagram debrief: they were barely accustomed to sharing profiles like DiSC® or the Myers-Briggs Type Indicator®. The Enneagram seemed like a step too far in the direction of "touchy-feely" personal disclosure, especially as the intended follow-up was to be a workshop to share their individual experiences and then reflect on one another's similarities and differences. For a group who preferred their prime language to be structure and logic, this proposed workshop was anxiety provoking.

The success of the workshop was partly due to the emotional intelligence of the executive leader, the owner. His willingness to share, and to show vulnerability in disclosing some of his insights from his Enneagram profile, made a visible impact on his team, and opened the way for authentic participation. He spoke of his astonishment at the accuracy of his profile: while briefly noting its observations of his positive qualities, he shared with humour the comments on his almost fanatic work ethic, his perfectionist drive, and poor tolerance for leisure activities, especially when the interaction was not about work. He hardly ever socialised with people from work unless they were entertaining a client. He reminded the team of how he had decided he wanted more connection with them after work. After all, he had recruited each of them, and had known several of them for years – yet lately, he had begun to be aware of the one-sidedness of *how* he knew them. So, he set about increasing his connection with his team like solving a mathematical problem. One day, seeing them gather together in a communal area after work, he left his office and went and sat among them. When he did this, the team grew silent and uncomfortable – their anxious glances with one another seemed to be asking what they had done to deserve this kind of surveillance. Gradually, over time, he felt able to contribute to those spontaneous social moments when they arose – to get curious, ask questions, share stories, be *human*. They were all now able to laugh at the recollection, and were touched when he told them it was their kindness to him, despite the awkwardness, that enabled him to loosen up and enjoy sharing banter.

His strongest Enneagram type was Type 1, the Perfectionist, as was another member of the team. While they shared some common characteristics, each had a different motivation for their type. The owner had had a deeply religious upbringing that stressed the sanctity of hard work. Lounging around with a drink in hand, sharing nothing of great importance with colleagues, seemed unconscionable. The other's motivation was a love of accuracy, which spilt over into a time-consuming obsession with detail. Both of them were hard on themselves, with a high degree of fear of failure, and a resulting tendency to be overly critical of others. A key learning for them was to learn to trust their already-high standards – that if they found something to be wrong, it was unlikely to be a disaster – and to balance being critical with giving recognition to employees they led for good intentions or for work well done.

When the Enneagram profile is made available to all members of a team, it facilitates discovery about colleagues, their default survival strategies, and blind spots. Feedback from a strong-willed team member, an Enneagram 8 with a forceful style and short on patience, shows that these insights can lead to better relationship awareness among team members and more skilful relationship management. After becoming familiar with his Enneagram profile, the Active Controller, he shared with his team-mates:

> I know now why I prefer working with some people more than others – I think they are more like me, on the same page, so together we can make things happen. And the others just have had to get on with it. It's been a big *aha* to realise that you, G … are not being deliberately difficult – you are picky about detail because that's your style – a Perfectionist. You obsess on getting things right, and I know now that you get anxious if you can't see all the pieces. Meanwhile, I'm just telling you to get on with it – so we've been clashing. Now I'm saying to myself, not to interrupt you, but give you time …

Quadrant questions to help you explore your Enneagram type

Having explained the four Integral quadrants and their meaning, each team member was asked to populate their quadrants, using the questions in each quadrant to explore their Enneagram type. Here are some of the questions based on the four quadrants that were used for participants to explore their Enneagram patterns, and then share their answers with their groups:

- *Upper-left quadrant – individual interior:*
  My thoughts and feelings:
    - How is my Enneagram type helping me understand my core nature?
    - What inspires me about my type? What concerns me?
    - What is the Enneagram confirming about how I think and feel?
    - What insights and understanding is my Enneagram type giving me about who I am?
    - What insights and understanding is my Enneagram type giving me about how I regard others?
- *Upper-right quadrant – individual exterior:*
  My behaviour, how I show up:
    - How is my Enneagram type helping me understand some of my behaviours, what I do or won't do, how I react, how I show up to others?
    - What am I aware of doing in my day-to-day interactions that I would like to change? Modify? Build on?
    - How will that show up?
    - What practices and skills would I like to change, build on?
- *Lower-left quadrant – collective interior:*
  Our communal space – collective shared values and emotional issues:
    - What is the impact of learning about the different Enneagram types of the members of our team/group?
    - How can we commit to better communication with one another?
    - What are our shared values and concerns?
    - How can knowledge of our Enneagram types help us support each other?
- *Lower-right quadrant – collective exterior:*
  Our outputs, systems, and processes – the impact on productivity:
    - How can our shared understanding of the Enneagram add value to what we do for the business?
    - Are we placing people in their best role in using their skills for the business?
    - What structures, practices, or processes would we consider modifying or changing?

Each participant in the architects' and designers' workshop was asked to review what they had written in each of the four quadrants and to make a list on a flipchart sheet of all the characteristics and qualities they valued about their own Enneagram type. There were eight individuals, representing among them seven of the nine Enneagram types. Each displayed their flipchart and read out their list. The invitation to the group listening was to make a note of the characteristics they enjoyed about their colleague and those they struggled with. By now, more than halfway through the day, the group had established a level of robust safety among themselves, and were willing to disclose to one another, trusting that the overall outcome was to create even stronger relationships. When a designer, who was Type 2, the Empathetic Helper, displayed his list of what he valued about his type in each of the quadrants, the Active Controller (Type 8) and the Driven Achiever (Type 3) commented on what had frustrated them in some of their colleague's patterns – especially the desire to connect with and help others, to be willing to listen to clients and juniors. At the same time, they were able to appreciate the value of a colleague having traits that they did not possess. They appreciated that their outcomes-driven focus sometimes overlooked compassion for others, leading to consequences for staff and clients. At the same time, the Empathetic Helper recognised that his need to be the helper was sometimes timewasting and not in the best interests of meeting deadlines, for which there might be a financial penalty. In the closing round of the day, the overarching comments were gratitude for insights into themselves and a better understanding of their colleagues. We agreed to meet for a follow-up in three months to take stock and evaluate the impact of this experience on internal and external relationships.

The importance of continuous practice

It must be emphasised that teams need to frequently revisit their individual and group profiles on-the-job, building on their insights and enhancing emotional robustness in the consideration of every new client, every project plan discussion, and the evaluation of every project completion. Without constant ongoing reflection with reference to these interlocking approaches (in this methodology, Wilber's quadrants, meeting management skills, and tools like the Enneagram profiles), people are highly likely to default to their more embedded and less conscious behaviours. It is tiring to practise self-awareness and initiate self-management actions. Until this new work becomes second nature, it takes effort to bring attention to relationships, and even more effort to improve the quality of our ways of engaging with others. The ultimate aim is self-awareness resulting in effective emotionally robust teamwork, which "happens best in a *psychologically safe* workplace where people are not inhibited by interpersonal fear" (Edmondson, 2019: location 349).

Establishing psychological safety

Edmondson (2019) makes an important distinction between trust and psychological safety in teams and organisations. Both concepts are desirable, but each functions differently. Trust is a subjective, interpersonal condition that exists in the mind of an individual. Psychological safety is established when there is a company-wide commitment to truthful observations if they are made in the interests of the business, no matter how awkward or troublesome they appear to be. Establishing psychological safety does not mean having to relax performance standards; on the contrary, having a company culture that encourages employees to raise concerns, even if they turn out to be wrong, strengthens performance. It overcomes a tendency for team members to be "nice" rather than raise uncomfortable issues, especially to one's manager. Building psychological safety encourages everyone to focus on outcomes that matter to the success of the team or the business. It is about accountability, holding people to agreed goals and outcomes (Edmondson 2019: location 17). As a leader, being aware of and sharing one's own Enneagram patterns with those of one's team or group has the potential to dismantle conflict and build the psychological safety needed for robust discussions.

If you haven't already done it, it is well worth completing an Enneagram questionnaire from a reputable company, and having a certified Enneagram coach or consultant debrief it with you – and making this available as a team exercise. It is important to emphasise that such an exercise should not be regarded as a fun break from the office, but as an ongoing process of raising awareness, enhancing emotional intelligence, building connections, and managing relationships skilfully.

Chapter 8 is an introduction to evolving worldviews and adult stages of development, and their relevance for leaders in a VUCA world.

Chapter 8

Onwards and upwards
Leadership and stages of adult development

The importance of psychological safety

Imagine a situation where a senior manager is promoted to the Executive Committee of a fast-evolving international company. The promotion in this complex multi-cultural and multinational environment demands higher levels of autonomy, resilience, and inventiveness under pressure. The new work environment, as well as the onset of the COVID-19 pandemic, requires an increased level of complexity greater than this individual can meet. The CEO and fellow ExCo members become increasingly frustrated as they keep fixing incomplete projects on behalf of their colleague. She senses their annoyance covered over with "niceness" and, in turn, feels anxious and resentful. Nothing about her underperformance is ever really clearly and openly discussed with her until, finally, there is an angry and abusive explosion from the CEO in front of colleagues in an ExCo meeting.

This scenario, which in my experience has occurred frequently in one form or another, raises the enormous value of having the robust conditions for a *psychologically safe* environment, described in Chapter 6. Maintaining such an environment emphasises the importance of being able to have tough but crucial conversations (Glaser, 2014), and especially being aware of the impact of the *language* leaders use. Kegan and Lahey (2001: 8) argue that "In our view, leaders have no choice in this matter of being language leaders; it just goes with the territory. ... The only question is what kind of language leaders we will be."

The way a person is treated by their manager when confronted with issues like poor performance, lack of integrity, and disappointing values will determine whether they are willing to engage positively and with accountability in reflecting on their performance, or alternatively shut down defensively (Rock, 2008). When we are spoken to negatively, we are more focused on the way we are treated and how we *feel* rather than *really hearing* and considering the issue that is being raised. Lisa Feldman Barrett (2020: 90) tells us that words "are tools for regulating human bodies. Other people's words have a direct effect on your brain activity and your bodily systems."

A wealth of emergent research shows just how much we affect one another in relationships. David Rock recognised the importance of just how we affect

DOI: 10.4324/9781003377221-9

one another when he decided to draw on limbic brain research for his doctorate (completed in 2007). He believed that it was important for a wider audience than scientists and neurologists to have access to fast-emerging and increasingly exciting findings on the workings of our brain and the effect we have on one another. His research led him to create his immensely successful brain-based model, SCARF®. The acronym stands for Status, Certainty, Autonomy, Relatedness, and Fairness, each being key triggers to reactions in the brain in response to the way we are treated. Depending on whether these key triggers are stimulated positively or negatively, the limbic area of the brain generates the appropriate release of neurochemicals and hormones into the body – fight, flight, or freeze reactions if negatively stimulated, or a warm, approachable, welcoming response if positively stimulated (Rock, 2008). Amanda Blake (2018: location 129) confirms, in the introduction to her aptly named book, *Your Body Is Your Brain*, that it is a mistake to imagine "our minds are separate from our bodies", an observation for which there is increasing evidence from fellow researchers. By 2012, just five years later, Rock's SCARF® model had reached "hundreds of thousands of people" and was widely discussed in management circles, apparently considered one of the "Best Ideas of 15 Years" by *Business+Strategy* magazine (Rock and Cox, 2012: 1).

For coaches and leaders-as-coach, working with the SCARF® model is an accessible way to understand just how devastating negative behaviours can be in affecting productivity. If one of the five SCARF® buttons is triggered, it can set off a chain reaction with all five – like a set of dominoes. Having a superior demean one's worth or *status* can result in an individual feeling *uncertain*; *autonomy* may be undermined, especially if one is micromanaged, with a growing sense of powerlessness, and the victim is sadly adrift in their capacity to *relate* positively; and it simply does not feel *fair*. Conversely, an emotionally intelligent leader can raise energy and inspire positivity by skilfully and appropriately reinforcing these five triggers.

Halfway through the coaching project with AMSA, the unit was threatened by a merger, an entire makeover of the lower-right quadrant: systems, structures, roles, legal frameworks, etc. The merger initiative collapsed at the eleventh hour, but until then, all the five responses described by David Rock were negatively triggered – upper-left quadrant and lower-left quadrant activity. The *status* of the CEO and his executive managers would be undermined by having to swim with very much bigger fish in a completely different and hostile sea; there was no *certainty* either about the fate of all the employees at AMSA or about the timelines involved; *autonomy* to lead the company into the future was suspended; there was little chance of being able to *relate* empathetically to the key players in this proposed merger; and above all, the secrecy, lack of information, and sudden prospect of a possible bleak future felt very *unfair*. (A quick and easy introduction to this powerful model can be found in NeuroLeadership Institute, 2022.)

Horizontal and vertical development

The skills to master the interlocking leadership competencies that result in a sturdy, but psychologically safe environment require continuous self-awareness and reflective practice – to borrow from Kegan-Lahey terminology, a *deliberatively developmental* approach (Kegan and Lahey, 2016), or put another way, an organisation committed from the top to encouraging both *horizontal and vertical development*.

Human development from childhood and throughout adulthood depends upon both horizontal and vertical evolution. Horizontal development enables individuals to become better, more skilful, at building on what they already do, while vertical development describes potential access to an expanding, increasingly more complex range of worldviews. Imagine, for example, an apprentice electrician becoming a master electrician over the course of a working life (horizontal development), and who is satisfied with and unquestioning of their worldview and range of cultural values (vertical level). If this same individual shifts from a narrow belief in only one way to socialise and one cultural group to connect with, to an open-hearted curiosity in social practices and cultural groups other than their own, that would indicate a mindset/worldview shift – in other words, vertical development: the ability to become aware of and engage with more complexity, a wider range of experiences and interests.

In Chapter 5, I mention a coaching colleague in the Texas "Bible Belt" who, after decades of conformity to the values of his close-knit community, in mid-life began to explore other forms of spiritual practice, including Buddhism. He was rejected by his community as a result of his growing interest in various beliefs and forms of spiritual practice. He himself explained his steadfast commitment to enlarging his sphere of knowledge and experience of religious principles and practices, in spite of rejection by his community, as an increased curiosity that he could not resist. He described a feeling of restlessness and frustration in his community that initially he could not explain, but gradually the feeling manifested in an insatiable desire to explore the world of faith beyond his narrow body of knowledge and experience. He realised that he had experienced a mindset shift, a vertical shift, an expansion in perspective-taking that had been fulfilling for him and that also enabled him to accept with equanimity the rupture between his community and himself.

Horizontal development is equally as important as vertical growth, and may even accelerate a mindset shift. At present, horizontal competency is the area of development most emphasised in the workplace. Organisations are very familiar with horizontal typologies which differentiate between styles or types, but which in the main offer no indication of the range of complexity available to each individual within their preferred style. Horizontal typologies like the Myers-Briggs Type Indicator®, StrengthsFinder®, DiSC®, and Insights® indicate personality types or learning style preferences present *at any stage* of adult development. An illustration of horizontal typing is the "communications styles" questionnaire that classifies four preferred styles – action-oriented, people-oriented, process-oriented, or ideas-oriented. These preferences for a communication style do not, however, indicate the *stage* of development of a particular individual. In other words, they tell us nothing about the particular mindset or worldview of an individual. Jones, Chesley, and Egan cite research suggesting that most leaders lack an understanding of mental complexity and the focus needed to increase vertical development, "creating a gap between the leadership we have and the leadership we need for the future" (Jones, Chesley, and Egan, 2020: 2), a gap that under current world pressures will increase.

A brief background to vertical growth – stages of adult development

In the 1950s, the psychologist Clare Graves proposed that "the psychology of the mature human being is an unfolding, emergent, oscillating, spiralling process marked by progressive subordination of older, lower-order behaviour systems to newer, higher-order systems as an individual's existential problems change" (Beck and Cowan, 2000: 28). Subsequently, Graves' conjectures led to the concept of *construct development*, the term that describes the potential for adults to take on new and more complex constructs of themselves and their world through the course of their lives. Not only do individual adults hold the potential to grow through these stages of development towards greater, more conscious complexity; cultures and nations also have the potential to evolve in increasingly complex ways. This holds immense significance for the field of leadership.

There are many different stage conceptions with nominal levels, depending on what aspect of development is being evaluated. Jean Piaget (1896–1980) developed his seminal work in the mid-twentieth century on his four stages of child development, until which time there was no theory of normal child development. The awareness of child stages of development has brought significant changes to legislation in the protection of children. It also ushered in preferred ways in which children should now be raised and educated.

Lawrence Kohlberg (1927–1987), who admired Piaget's approach to stages in the development of children, described six levels of response from children to adults to a moral dilemma contained in a little story. In listening to their reasoning, he demonstrated how moral judgement evolves from a response based on self-interest in young children and the low end of adult development (preconventional), to a concern for justice for society as a whole in young and mature adults (post-conventional). His most well-known moral dilemma story is about Heinz, an adult, who steals a drug. Heinz learns that his wife has a serious disease from which she will die if she does not have access to a certain drug. He asks his pharmacist for the drug, but it is too expensive for him to be able to pay for it, and the pharmacist refuses to allow him to pay the cost in instalments. He decides the next night to break into the pharmacy and steal the drug to save his wife's life. The question is: was Heinz right or wrong to steal the drug? After analysing several hundred interviews, Kohlberg charted six stages of moral development from simple reasons why Heinz should or should not have stolen the drug, through to very sophisticated reasoning (Boeree, 2009).

The breakthrough thinking by Piaget and Kohlberg was their concept of and evidence for stages of consciousness development, evolving from simple to complex. Up to 50 years ago, there was no accepted psychological theory of "normal" adult development. The entry of psychology as a field of study of human behaviour focused on pathology – "abnormal" adult behaviour. The interest in and rigorous study of normal adult development is relatively new, though intimations of the need for this area of academic enquiry were already emergent 70 years ago.

"Transcend and include"

Growth in vertical stages of adult development results in an increase in complexity and perspective-taking that *transcends and includes* the capacity of each of the previous stages. Core to the understanding of vertical growth is the concept of *transcend and include*, explained by Wilber in many of his books: "Each stage of evolution (human or otherwise) transcends and includes its predecessors. Atoms are parts of molecules, which are parts of cells, which are part of complex organisms, and so on" (Wilber, 2001b: 66–67).

Another example is letters which are parts of words which are parts of sentences. Levels or stages build on their predecessors in concrete ways: a baby must crawl before walking. A world-class tennis player has mastered complex physical skills that *transcend* the ability to crawl in infancy – though if they had to, they could no doubt *include* crawling in their physical repertoire. Human beings spend many hours of every day practising to acquire skills in order to develop successive, more complex stages. A key consideration for organisational culture and for the leader-as-coach is that no person can jump to more complex stages of development without growing sequentially through their own stages.

The American psychologist Abraham Maslow (1908–1970) could be said to be the first in his field to study mentally healthy individuals, which led to the first publication of his theory of the *hierarchy of human needs* in 1943. In later publications, he constructed a model comprising a pyramid of five layers of human needs. The lowest level represents physiological needs, meeting the need to survive from day to day, an all-consuming task, unless one can ascend to the next level, which is having safety (e.g. the security of having a job). Once that level of security is established, the need for love, companionship, and connection can be met. Thereafter, the need for respect and recognition might arise, before the emergence of the fifth level, self-actualisation. Towards the end of his life, he believed there was a sixth level above self-actualisation – self-transcendence (Maslow, 2011). In the last years of his life, he corrected the original impression, from his description of his hierarchy, that needs must be satisfied in a given order – shifting from the lowest level of fundamental survival needs to the next higher-order needs. Though he maintained that thwarting a need at one level could cause stress and inhibit access to functioning at the level above, he later acceded that remaining at a particular level for someone might be a choice.

Table 8.1 First tier of value levels in business, in individuals, in human evolution

Value levels	Business levels	Individual waves	Human evolution
Beige	Concern for the next few months only.	Basic survival – shelter, eating, sleeping, etc.: egocentric.	Early cave man.
Purple	Company seen as "family".	Loyalty to the tribe – sociocentric.	Tribal formations.
Red	Aggressively territorial, there can be one boss only, zero-sum game rules.	Fight for what you want – egocentric.	Survival in the jungle – winner takes all.
Blue	Conservative, rule-bound, hierarchical.	Rules make life secure – sociocentric.	Order out of chaos – God is on our side.
Orange	Entrepreneurial – profit-driven, decisions made in business interests only.	Look after No 1 – the world is my oyster – egocentric.	Technology, mobility, global capitalism.
Green	Team-based co-created, embracing triple-bottom-line focus – financial, human development, and social responsibility.	Consultative, caring.	Age of consciousness moving to worldcentric.

Source: Aiken (2009: 28), adapted from Beck and Cowan (2000).

Regarding human consciousness development, the realm of the upper-left quadrant, six to ten basic structural levels or stages have been described, depending on the researcher: for example, Wilber describes ten stages; Susanne Cook-Greuter names eight; David Rooke and Bill Torbert name seven; and Robert Kegan works with five. Each researcher in stage development describes the movement from less complexity, less perspective-taking, and more certainty, to more complexity, more ability to hold multiple perspectives, and an increased tolerance for managing ambiguity. Don Beck and Christopher Cowan (2000), students of the late Clare Graves, colour-coded these levels, called *memes*, in their seminal work, *Spiral Dynamics: Mastering Values, Leadership and Change*. Each colour represents a particular set of values, a particular way of viewing and behaving in the world. Table 8.1 offers a brief description of these colour codes and their levels.

First-tier and second-tier levels – subsistence versus being

Clare Graves describes the first six levels of consciousness as *First Tier's Subsistence Levels*. Between these and the emergence of *Second Tier's Being Levels* is a "momentous leap" for which, Graves (1974) conjectures, human nature is being prepared, levels which introduce "a complexity beyond even the best First Tier thinking" (Beck and Cowan, 2000: 274). A characteristic of the six levels at first tier is that each level at its own stage of development tends to be critical of the levels from which it has emerged, and largely oblivious to emergent levels. For example, an organisation or nation run by a single autocratic "might-is-right" leader (coded Red in Table 8.1) is considered an advance on, and more efficient than, the "all for one, one for all – and don't stick your head above the parapet" view at traditional community level (Purple). An organisation with a board of directors, a body of executives, and a chain of command representing a pyramid-type body of authority (Blue) where rules and traditions are honoured, considers itself an advance on the Red order (Beck and Cowan, 2000). The significant difference of second-tier consciousness and its implications for twenty-first-century leadership is the (still rare) ability to understand and engage appropriately with all levels at first tier.

Significantly for leadership, these levels of human consciousness and perspective-taking are, probably for the first time in human history, all evidential and present simultaneously across the world. According to Frédéric Laloux in his book, *Reinventing Organisations: A Guide to Creating Organisations Inspired by the Next Stage of Human Consciousness*:

> Never before in human history have we had people operating from so many different paradigms all living alongside each other. The same is true for organisations: in the same city, if we care to look, we can find Red, Amber, Orange, and Green organisations working side by side.
>
> (Laloux, 2014: 35)

Indeed, all these levels also may be found *within a single organisation*, which is highly significant for the overall performance of an organisation and its inclusion of leadership development at every level.

The upper-left quadrant – the space of emerging consciousness

The territory of the upper-left quadrant is the site of human consciousness evolution – the individual subjective capacity for increasing awareness. Jane Loevinger (1918–2008) and more recently, building on Loevinger's work, Susanne Cook-Greuter designed sentence completion tests which provide evidence that an individual conceives of, and is conscious of, different values at each level of expanding complexity. For example, when asked to complete the sentence *"A good marriage is ... "*, at the pre-modern stage an individual might respond " *... when the man is the head of the household and each family member knows their place"*. A postmodern and more complex response to completing the same sentence might be " *... when a couple develop a lifelong friendship based on equality and respect for each other's differences"* (Simcox, 2005).

The practice of cultivating awareness within any stage is the key factor to enable stage growth in adults, and movement from one stage to another is a gradual process. Encouraging news from Rooke and Torbert (2005: 7), who use the term "action logic" in their research rather than speaking of stages or levels, is that within one or two years, "leaders can transform from one action logic to another". However, Cook-Greuter (1994: 121) points out that "most growth in adulthood seems to occur *within* a given stage, i.e., *laterally*." Cook-Greuter also notes that the capacity for horizontal development increases exponentially at more advanced stages of development.

The main characteristics of the first six stages of consciousness in the first tier of adult development can be described as follows:

- *The Opportunist* is characterised by deep self-interest and self-gratification – the lack of self-awareness and perspective-taking is unlikely to be found at the management level in this workshop environment. The Opportunist reacts to feedback as aggression, a threat.
- *The Diplomat* demonstrates a need to conform to rules and norms – their strong need to belong shows itself in loyalty, and their downside is rudeness and rejection of anyone or anything outside their view of the one true way. The Diplomat can react with shame at receiving feedback, seeing it as negative judgement, failure.
- *The Expert* thrives on being respected for knowledge and skills, and takes pride in being acknowledged as expert. This person tends to conform with rules and regulations, and is attentive to detail, but, on the downside, has a need to be seen as right – there is a tendency to be a rigid and controlling leader. The Expert reacts to criticism by taking it personally; there is a tendency to dismiss the opinions of others not seen as expert in their field.
- *The Achiever* seeks opportunities to succeed, and strives to meet self-selected standards. They show good problem-solving ability, and value achieving outcomes with others. Their triggers are being restricted by hierarchy and being forced to comply with what does not make sense. The Achiever is happy to accept feedback that helps them achieve their goals.
- *The Individualist* demonstrates a desire to find meaning and purpose; they enjoy having individuality, in exploring new ideas, and are open to new perspectives. They are capable of recognising bias in others and in themselves. Their triggers are being limited by colleagues who have an over-reliance on "fact" and logic, who can see only one perspective, and who take a strong stand on issues. The Individualist welcomes feedback, especially the insight it gives them into their own behaviour.
- *The Strategist* shows an ability to hold multiple perspectives, and accepts conflict as an inevitable aspect of human relations. They are willing to reframe a situation, and willing to test the practical application of good theory. They may appear arrogant and "knowing". The Strategist seeks out and enjoys feedback as self-development (Simcox, 2005).

A sample survey enabled the proportion of adults in the general US population occupying each of the above stages in 1999 to be estimated as follows: Opportunists, 4.3 per cent; Diplomats, 11.3 per cent; Experts, 36.5 per cent; Achievers, 29.7

per cent; Individualists, 11.3 per cent; Strategists and above 6.9 per cent (Cook-Greuter 2004: 279).

At each level of the first tier, individuals tend to be unaware of the stages that potentially lie ahead until they become frustrated with the limits of their current worldview – and then become dismissive of the stage from which they have emerged. The child who just yesterday believed in Father Christmas feels smug and superior to their "silly" younger sibling for being a believer today. As we develop to each successive stage, we increasingly grow our knowledge: the ability to notice more, recognise patterns, understand rules, see further into the future, make connections back in time, and accomplish more. As we become more developed, we acquire wisdom as well as knowledge, showing an increasing depth of understanding, and being able to recognise and question assumptions; we become more self-aware, more reflective, increasingly capable of seeing system dynamics, and stripped of illusions.

Susanne Cook-Greuter has since updated and renamed the labels of each of these stages, with specific reference to stages of leadership maturity, to obviate the possible judgement perceived in words like "opportunist" and "expert" (see Figure 8.1). Her diagram represents 80–85 per cent of leaders on the spectrum of increasing knowledge, from the least (Self-Centric) at bottom left of the arc to the most (Self-Determining) at the crest of the arc; from the crest of the arc to the right is a movement showing the gradual acquisition of wisdom from self-questioning to unitive, representing a mere 15–20 per cent of leaders.

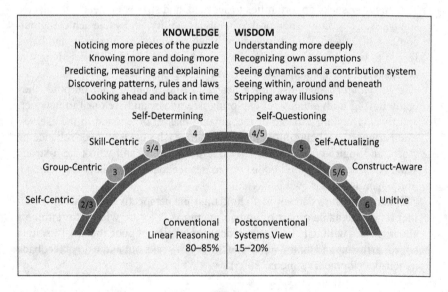

Figure 8.1 Leadership journey to wisdom: stages of leadership maturity. Source: Cook-Greuter (2018: 304).

A natural hierarchy, a dominator hierarchy, or no hierarchy

In traditional organisations and corporate structures, the higher up one is in the hierarchy, the more power and privilege one accrues – and, controversially, with power and privilege there is evidence of entitlement. In a *dominator hierarchy*, the notion of superiority, and therefore entitlement to privilege, as a consequence of increasing positional power, has been variously institutionally and systemically reinforced. In contrast, the notion of ever-more complex stages of reflective consciousness embraced in Integral vision does not incorporate an ideology of superiority or entitlement to power and privilege.

In a *natural hierarchy*, each increasing stage of adult development carries increasing responsibility for managing complexity. A natural hierarchy in an organisation is, in Integral vision, considered a more realistic and nuanced concept than the functioning of a flat organisation. "Unlike any other corporate structure that exists, flat companies are exactly that ... flat. Meaning there are usually no job titles, seniority, managers, or executives. Everyone is seen as equal" (Morgan, 2015: 2). While this value of *equality* may seem highly desirable, especially in relation to a repressive dominator hierarchy, it does not account for unequal stages or levels of development in employees – and the greater the number of employees, the more that unequal stage development matters.

As pointed out in Chapter 2, a healthy family, for example, might consist of two parents carrying more complexity and responsibility at their stage of development than their ten-year old child, or their three-year old with the least developed complexity. Each member, in a natural hierarchy, is included and valued *at their stage*. People at any stage in a family or an organisation are not ready for self-governing without the requisite conditions in place – conditions that include both behaviour and structures. Lloyd Chapman (2010: 30) observes,

> According to Jaques and Clement (1997), pathology enters the hierarchy and makes it dysfunctional when an individual occupies a role in which he or she does not possess the required cognitive complexity to match the required task complexity of that stratum of complexity. The problem is not the organisational hierarchy *per se* but the person occupying the managerial role.

Cognitive complexity is just one of several intelligences that should be at the appropriate level of development to match task complexity – a topic which will be described shortly.

There is no suggestion among exponents of human development (theorists like Abraham Maslow, Clare Graves, Don Beck and Christopher Cowan, Robert Kegan, Ken Wilber, Bill Torbert, or Susanne Cook-Greuter) that higher-order stages mean "better" people with a *carte blanche* entitlement to power and privilege. Wilber (2015) points out, for example, that the Machiavellian villain Darth Vader of the *Star Wars* films is a brilliant demonstration of highly developed complexity, well able to hold multiple perspectives – higher-order development does not automatically ensure utopia or guarantee the best of human behaviour. "The solution is not to condemn the hierarchy but to get rid of or develop the pathological holon within that hierarchy" (Chapman, 2010: 30).

An individual's expressed *values and beliefs* (upper-left quadrant) may be at a higher level of consciousness than the demonstrable level of their *actions and behaviours* (upper-right quadrant). For example, a client in the Human Resources talent development division of an international banking institution demonstrates the incongruence that can occur in a four-quadrant context at work. She does not believe in the value of the performance appraisal system, a twice-yearly event at which managers score the performance of their staff against set indicators. Both managers and their staff are stressed by the engagement, and many would prefer a more regular meeting throughout the year, managed as a flexible two-way conversation. She is, however, constrained by conservative company policies to conform to and uphold the outcomes of the rigid twice-a-year performance appraisal. Her mindset illustrates a flexible interactive approach encouraging a degree of autonomy in employees – an advance on strictly constraining a performance review to a rigid scoring system, where the dialogue in the encounter is entirely in the hands of the more senior person. Equally, someone who responds well to being given instruction may feel uncertain and anxious in a more advanced organisational culture that encourages a degree of autonomy. Laloux (2014: 41) makes the significant observation that

> Consciously or unconsciously, leaders put in place organisational structures, practices, and cultures that make sense to them, that correspond to their way of dealing with the world. This means that an organisation cannot evolve beyond its leadership's stage of development.

Worth bearing in mind are two key factors: the *range of worldviews* (or stages, mindsets) to which we have access, and our *centre of gravity*. Wilber (2001b) describes "centre of gravity" as the dominant mindset of an individual, and emphasises the wave-like access we have to other stages that we have exceeded – remembering that as we grow and develop, in childhood and in adulthood, we *transcend* a stage and *include* it in the more expanded stage we have achieved. We can also peak in more complex stages of which we have glimpses, and then fall back to the dominant mindset. The fact that a leader has achieved the highest mindset stage is not necessarily an indication or a guarantee that they are an effective, successful leader. According to Petrie (2020: 8), based on research of the consequences for leadership, "The clearest pattern we saw was that leaders who displayed the *most vertical range* were the ones most likely to be high performers." These are leaders who are learning to have access to and awareness of types other than their own dominant pattern. Petrie (2020: 12) found that "Leaders love the idea of range because it doesn't put them in 'a box' and is much closer to their lived experience."

What follows here is a guide to increasing awareness by paying attention to a particular range of intelligences within the scope of every normally functioning adult – "normal" in this context meaning no brain damage. Practising attention to particular lines of intelligence in the course of an ordinary day can lead to increased self-awareness sufficient to change a perception, a course of action, an entire perspective – leading to a shift in vertical development.

A practical guide to advancing vertical development – working with six lines of intelligence

There are claims that we have the potential for upward of 23 kinds of intelligence, including categories like mathematical, musical, aesthetic, or spatial intelligence. Not all these intelligences are relevant to each of us in the fulfilment of our potential; we don't all need to be mathematically articulate or musically skilful. Nonetheless, according to Wilber, at least six of these lines of intelligence are available to, and necessary for, the normally functioning adult.

Each of these six lines of intelligence, referred to as a *psychograph* by Wilber and illustrated in Figure 8.2, has the potential for three general levels of increasing ability to hold complexity – low or preconventional, medium or conventional, and high or postconventional (Wilber, 2001b: 24–25). Each of these individual lines shows its own stages of progressive development. Also, each stage along these lines of development has its light and shadow, its healthy aspects and pathological aspects. These lines of intelligence develop relatively independently of one another, though they are intertwined. Most of us tend to excel along one or two of these lines, and perform less well on the others.

Practising these six intelligences gives adults access to a greater range of their awareness. A brief explanation of each of the six lines of intelligence follows:

1. *Cognitive intelligence* has the increasing ability to hold multiple sources of information, more than one point of view or perspective, and see their implications and evaluate alternative scenarios into the future. The low end of cognitive development has a concern for concrete reality, here and now, with little awareness or imagination for the future. The high end of cognitive

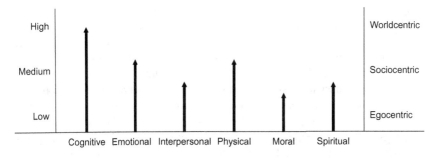

Figure 8.2 Lines and stages of development. Source: Adapted from Wilber (2000: 30).

development has the capacity to see multiple perspectives, and appreciate the value, synergies, and potential of those perspectives.

2. *Emotional intelligence* is the increasing ability to develop care and concern, as well as being able to manage emotional responses and use them constructively. We all start life in childhood at the egocentric level: with poor self-control, the focus of attention must be on *me*, the only important one. Some adults, it seems, never grow their emotional quotient any further. The middle range of emotional intelligence is *sociocentric* – care and concern for "me and people like me". Experts in this field of research that suggests that 78 per cent of adults across the globe are in this sociocentric category regardless of education, wealth or rural-versus-urban access. The world-centric level of emotional intelligence is the ability to include "me, my tribe *and* my enemy" with care and concern. Very few adults across the globe truly *embody* world-centric emotional intelligence, adept at self-reflection and self-insight, capable of courageous, creative tactics. An example is Nelson Mandela, who showed the capacity to access, communicate, and skilfully be present with care and concern for "me, my tribe and my enemy" in the interests of a peaceful transition from apartheid in South Africa.

3. *Interpersonal intelligence* is the increasing ability to accept difference with equanimity in those to whom one relates; it is the capacity to relate to and communicate with others in ways focusing on what motivates others, working co-operatively with others, and showing flexibility in social situations. The low end of interpersonal intelligence is characterised by poor conflict management, and poor awareness of the feelings and needs of others; while they can work well alone, they tend to be poor team players. In comparison, the high end of interpersonal intelligence reframes conflict as an opportunity to evaluate and appreciate both sides.

4. *Physical intelligence* manifests as an increasing awareness of one's physical being and the physical environment; it is the physical and mental fitness of being able to stay alert to a number of stimuli, both internally and externally. A good example of the high end of physical intelligence is a world-class athlete at the top of their game, with unswerving focus on the challenges they face. The parallel for a high-functioning leader is the ability to maintain core focus while simultaneously being aware of multiple issues, the ability to manage stress and know when and how to replenish energy.

5. *Moral intelligence* at the low end is dominated by "I win – you lose" values, with little or no care for the consequences to others; an example is Bernie Madoff, who used a Ponzi scheme to defraud thousands of investors who put their trust in him. The high end of moral intelligence is an increasing concern to act in the best interests of all, preserving the greatest value for all. The capacity to reach a moral decision involving both moral judgment and care increases from a focus on "me" to "us" to "all of us", and then to all sentient beings. At the leadership level, high-functioning moral intelligence displays kindness and fairness while being unafraid to take any necessary action in the interests of all, the greater good.

6. *Spiritual intelligence* at the low end is characterised by a fundamentalist belief in "one truth", unable to contemplate and intolerant of other versions of spiritual meaning. Any desire to serve is restricted to a small, identifiable group of like-minded members. Spiritual development incrementally moves to a growing sense of multiple ways to value life, resolving in an increasing recognition of the interconnectedness of all sentient life, and indeed, all matter on our planet and beyond. As leaders, they exude a calming presence that gives others a feeling of inclusivity and value.

How to choose your practice

Choose one or two lines on which to focus at any one time. Design an activity which will bring each of these lines into your conscious attention. On a daily basis, bring awareness to your practice, keep a journal, and reflect on what you are noticing. For example, if your focus is to increase your development on the interpersonal line, you might start by being aware of your voice of judgment in the presence of opinions (or dress codes, values, cultures, or races) that differ from your own. On the emotional line, perhaps you could notice, when driving in your car, or standing in a queue at a crowded supermarket, how often you feel judgmental and intolerant of others around you – egocentric (my needs now!) rather than sociocentric (we're in this together). In time you should find with regular practice that you are aware *in the moment* of a pattern, and in time, you should be able to consciously adjust your reaction or your behaviour to a more considered response.

Case study: The story of Malcolm and two managers – working with interpersonal intelligence

Malcolm had been with his company for ten years. Increasingly noted for his technical financial intelligence, and particularly his ability to recognise patterns and implications beyond the scope of a project, he was nurtured and encouraged by his boss, Manager A, to refine his ability to see complex cause-and-effect patterns and consider this his niche in the business.

Malcolm had a reputation for being difficult. Feedback comments from 360° surveys indicated that while he was wonderful with junior staff, and at mentoring younger or more inexperienced team members, he was impatient with peers, senior executives, and stakeholders whom he considered less knowledgeable than himself. Also, fixated on the solutions he had found, he was intolerant of entertaining alternative perspectives. His poor level of control in managing his emotions, especially when dealing with senior managers and stakeholders who were less technically competent, had been commented on several times.

Manager A, who realised Malcolm's unsociable conduct would stand in the way of others appreciating his value to the business, suggested to Malcolm that he try coaching to raise awareness of his behaviour at work and perhaps, as a result, be able to change his pattern. Conversations with Malcolm and his manager, as well as studying the range of comments in his 360° appraisals, gave me a sense of what

Malcolm's psychograph might look like (his level of development on each of the six lines of intelligence discussed above):

1. *Cognitive intelligence* – medium: though he had a complex combination of pattern-recognition and pattern-making, he did not easily accommodate opposing viewpoints, especially when they were not grounded in intelligent, verifiable data.
2. *Emotional intelligence* – medium: Malcolm was able to tolerate constructive criticism from a respected colleague or expert and was reasonably aware of his emotions, but was not sufficiently aware in the moment of the triggers of his negative behaviour and the impact he had on others.
3. *Interpersonal intelligence* – low: he was perceived by some of his peers and stakeholders as overly aggressive, not a good team-player. By his own admission, he saw interaction with a group where he was presenting a strategy as a game for him to win at all costs. His lack of awareness of the feelings, perceptions, and needs of others resulted in miscommunications, resulting in an inclination by others to doubt the value of his contribution.
4. *Physical intelligence* – low: Malcolm was very physically driven – a motor-bike rider, windsurfer, and runner – all high-intensity activities when he could find time to fit them in around the many long hours he worked evenings and weekends. He walked leaning forward, was breathless from talking too fast, and while he was aware of feeling physical strain, he did not seem able to pace himself.
5. *Moral intelligence* – medium to high: Malcolm tended to respect the social order in the organisation; he had a well-developed sense of fairness, showing care especially for junior staff and for those who were struggling. In his commitment to his work, he sought to make strategic decisions that were fair and lawful for the organisation. However, he still needed to learn to develop an equanimity to challenges and points of view he considered below standard.
6. *Spiritual intelligence* – medium heading towards high: Malcolm demonstrated having a strong purpose in life, and an increasing belief in the interconnectedness of all living forms. He expressed an open-hearted acceptance of a range of spiritual beliefs and practices.

Malcolm's coaching focused primarily on encouraging his reflection on his lowest lines – the *physical* and *interpersonal*. Through asking him to reflect and journal, he began to be aware of his level of physical strain, but it took some time for him to notice in the moment and intervene in his pattern. He was asked to be aware continuously of tension in his body, noticing when and where it was triggered. Gradually he learned to recognise and anticipate situations which caused him strain. He practised consciously breathing more deeply, dropping his shoulders, and pausing before rushing to speak. It was still very difficult for him not to interrupt someone, especially when he decided he did not value their contribution. The constant reminder to bring his focus into his body started to have a positive impact on his interpersonal awareness: as he learned to bring his attention into himself, notice, and pause, he recognised that he was achieving a calmer interaction with stakeholders and colleagues.

The coaching journey was slow going, with two steps forward, one back. Six months into the coaching journey, his boss noted in a performance review on Malcolm's behavioural skills:

> you have quite a long way to go in many of the development areas we identified last time.
> … You are sometimes a difficult person to work with. … I know you've been working hard at this, and I'd like to thank you for that. … If you keep working on it, the feedback will get better and better. Sometimes people take time to notice.

Referring to the Integral quadrants, Manager A went on to point out that Malcolm needed to work with the perspective of others (the lower-left quadrant – improving his interpersonal intelligence), and to manage frustration rather than become emotional (upper-left quadrant). He was criticised for being aggressive and insensitive to people – not in a malicious way – but the effect was nevertheless still harmful. Key development areas in Malcolm's behaviour that continued to detract from his strengths were ways in which he communicated (upper-right quadrant – physical and interpersonal intelligences). "Learn to relax. Tell others what they need to know, not what you want them to hear" was the advice of Manager A, himself highly emotionally intelligent and relationally skilful. Notice his affirming and appreciative comments to Malcolm, while not dodging the critical behavioural issues.

Encouraged by the highly supportive yet demanding relationship with his boss, Malcolm took his coaching tasks to heart. A plus in his ability to modify his behaviours in the business was his changed reaction to criticism. He had started to take it on without hostility, and with a desire to understand. He gradually increased his ability to see himself and reflect on what had happened in an interaction – as Robert Kegan (1994) puts it, *the subject becomes the object of his own awareness*. He was increasingly able to intervene in the moment in reframing his own knee-jerk reactions.

After 18 months, his second annual performance review since he started coaching indicated he was more than capable of consciously holding new behaviours in his awareness. Though he was never going to be perfect, he was now being complimented on his improved communications. Then, three years later, his exemplary boss left the company.

Under his newly promoted boss, Manager B, who had just recently been Malcolm's peer and who had not had a good relationship with him, things began to unravel for Malcolm. As I had been his coach during Manager A's tenure, on his own initiative he requested a meeting with me, in advance of which he sent me a letter to him from his new boss, which stated in part:

Delia [a member of Malcolm's team] is leaving us and has named you as a factor. This does not look good for you, and I will try and ensure that this is not a point captured in her exit interview. Whether she does or she doesn't name you, HR has got four prior employees who have listed you as a reason for their departure. I was not here at the time so I cannot comment on that. All I can say is that it is on your record and it does not look good.

What language do you notice in this manager's letter? How does he position himself? How supportive do you think he feels towards his direct report? As it happened, HR did not have evidence from four prior employees naming Malcolm as the reason for their departure. Both Malcolm and his current boss lacked sufficient incentive to improve interpersonal skills with respect to their mutual relationship. Consequently, they were on a collision course that ultimately resulted in Malcolm resigning.

Malcolm and I met for coffee mornings occasionally over the next few years. He established his own consultancy, and maintained his personal practice from his coaching sessions of journaling his reflections, particularly on his relationship management. His ability to withhold a counterproductive knee-jerk reaction with a difficult client was not simply because his income depended on it, but because he had recognised that he could observe a client's behaviour without feeling triggered by it: "I listen and try to respond to what the person really needs, not how they are acting out. And it works, it gets easier." Malcolm's willingness to be self-aware and practise changing his behaviour in the moment had led to a step up in his vertical development range, and an increase in interpersonal intelligence.

Conclusion

Research and recently published literature cited in this chapter and elsewhere in the book tells us that leadership development through an Integral lens, focusing on vertical learning, requires a significantly different approach from traditional leadership development with its emphasis on particular traits and a focus on process, systems, and structures. Trait- or character-based notions of what makes an effective leader will not be sufficient for effective – let alone transformational – leadership. Increasing evidence shows that helping leaders increase their range of complexity, the domain of vertical development theory, provides the means to close the development gap (Jones, Chesley, and Egan, 2020.)

There is one word which links the chapters and their stories throughout the book, one word that both kickstarts and underpins the methodology – *awareness*. Our implicit memory will trigger an interpretation or assumption of a current experience based on previous seemingly similar experiences, causing us to react in under a fifth of a second either positively or negatively – *unless* we can intervene consciously in this process. Conscious awareness of one's responses offers choices in intervening in the actions one might take. It suggests that nothing is more important for leadership at every level today than self-reflection and daily practices in developing awareness of one's own body, head, heart, soul, and spirit.

The need for vertical growth as a vital leadership capability has already emerged, with evidence of at least two such models already gaining attention in organisational literature – Robert Kegan's (1994) five stages of consciousness in adults, and Bill Torbert's (2004) eight stages or action logics. Recent publications like *Scaling Leadership* (Anderson and Adams, 2019) and *Agile Transformations* (Spayd and Madore, 2021) are examples of emergent practical guidelines for leaders who want to increase their vertical development.

Chapter 9 explores the use of polarity management to hold a "both-and" perspective rather than an "either-or" mindset as a means of resolving conflict.

Chapter 9

Revisiting "both-and"

Working with polarities

Development and conflict

Leaders with appropriate skills are needed at various levels within an organisation; the more complex the environment, the more capacity for complexity is required of a leader to be effective. Chapter 8 describes the concepts of horizontal and vertical development and the differences between them. We need to be conscious of development in both. However, effective leadership in a complex and fast-changing environment puts the emphasis on vertical growth and the development of particular capacities: to be reflective, to be self-aware, to open up to competing perspectives – and to manage *conflict* with equanimity.

In an ideal working world, employees would thrive in an environment that best represented their worldview, with leadership that connects with that worldview. There is a tendency in the variety of worldviews or mindsets described as *first tier* in Chapter 8 for each to be more committed to their own beliefs and opinions than interested in alternative viewpoints. A consequence is the likelihood of conflict as people take up opposing positions. A key characteristic of higher stages of leadership consciousness is access to and resilience in the face of complexity, the ability to hold multiple perspectives, and to recognise and appreciate differing mindsets for their potential to add value in the appropriate setting. A further defining characteristic of leadership capability is the effective management of conflict, and the skill of leading opposing factions to a resolution, co-created and generally accepted.

An important caveat: the words "lower" and "higher" with reference to adult development are problematic. Susanne Cook-Greuter (2004, 2005) emphasises the value of individuals at every phase of worldview or mindset development – no stage is better or worse than another, a perspective that has been endorsed by others (see for example Garvey Berger, 2019; Petrie, 2020). What matters is the appropriateness of a particular mindset to the situation in which an individual operates, and the leaders' abilities to recognise their own capacities and to understand the best fit for employees at different levels in their organisation.

DOI: 10.4324/9781003377221-10

Case study: The dilemma over Human Resources operations

A large media company with several subsidiaries had reached an impasse among its many directors. A debate raged over the most strategic, coherent, effective, and efficient approach for co-ordinating the range of functions of the various Human Resources units at head office and in the many subsidiaries nationally and internationally. And this was not the first time there had been furious head-butting over what the decision should be.

A decade earlier, the same debate had resulted in an agreement to decentralise Human Resources management, with head office and each subsidiary operating its own HR department. It seemed to make more sense that the roles of recruitment, training, compensating, and performance measurement, as well as core administrative functions like payroll management, would be more efficiently managed in localised domains. At great expense, the mammoth task was undertaken of downsizing the Human Resources department at head office, and instituting the skills and capacities for independent HR units in the subsidiaries.

Now, ten years after that restructuring, the heads of the various subsidiaries and the executives at head office were divided over the efficiencies of the decentralised arrangement. The managing director had announced a unilateral decision to centralise all HR functions back at head office. This unleashed a storm of conflict between those directors for and against, as well as fury at an independent decision being imposed from the top down without consultation.

The MD was persuaded, against his will, to organise a workshop to try to arrive at an agreement among all parties. As the facilitator of this three-day workshop process, my first task was to enable all voices to be clearly heard. With resistance from some of the participants, there was eventually an agreement to honour the conditions of a Thinking Environment® (described in Chapter 6). Even after the agreement was reached, there were some who found the process frustrating and inhibiting – the notion of each speaking once before anyone spoke twice, with no interruption and for an agreed amount of equally shared time, seemed infantile and controlling to them. Most others, fortunately, were keen to experience this approach to building a listening culture, even if it was temporary.

Either-or versus both-and

As the participants saw it, the issue to be resolved during the workshop was to agree *either* to re-centralise the Human Resources function at head office *or* to maintain the HR units as decentralised bodies.

The groundbreaking book *Polarity Management* by Barry Johnson (2014) recognises that some complex problems simply do not have either-or solutions. Johnson saw that problems of this type contained paradoxes and dilemmas –

polarities is his word for these complex factors. The basic message is that in a polarity, there is no one right answer and no simple solution. "The difficulty is the perception that (people) are dealing with a problem that can be solved by choosing either one or the other" (Johnson, 2014: 22). The resolution of a polarity arises from gathering in perspectives and opinions from all sides, and evaluating both the positive aspects and the limitations in each perspective. I proposed this process to the participants as a way to find a credible resolution that might be acceptable to everyone. Barry Johnson's methodology is remarkable not least for its inclusion of all levels, all perspectives of adult development, without judgement.

We set up a flipchart stand in each of the four corners of the room. Chart One focused on one pole, "The advantages of centralised HR"; Chart Two focused on the other pole, "The advantages of decentralised HR"; Chart Three was labelled "The disadvantages of centralised HR"; and Chart Four, "The disadvantages of decentralised HR" (see Figure 9.1). The participants were divided into four groups, and each group was requested to stand in front of one of the flipcharts and populate it with one-line summaries of their views. After an agreed period, each group rotated to the next flipchart, until each group had had an opportunity to populate every flipchart with their views.

	Centralised pole	Decentralised pole
Advantages	**Chart One** The advantages of centralised HR.	**Chart Two** The advantages of decentralised HR.
Disadvantages	**Chart Three** The disadvantages of centralised HR.	**Chart Four** The disadvantages of decentralised HR.

Figure 9.1 Use of a polarity map to clarify options. Source: Client data mapped according to the basic format used in Johnson (2014: 3–17).

Looking at the four flipcharts, side by side, it emerged that there were clearly valid views for both centralised and decentralised HR functions that had been found by *all* the participants. Polarity management suggests a way of honouring and embracing the outcomes of both poles. The participants had come together to create a list of the advantages and disadvantages *in both positions*.

The next task was for them to work out how to maximise the positive aspects of both centralised and decentralised systems: "to gain and maintain the benefits of one pole, you must also pursue the benefits of the other" (Johnson, 2014: 23). For each positive outcome listed on the flipcharts, action steps needed to be designed, setting out ways of gaining or maintaining positive results from a focus on this pole, naming what was to be done, by whom, and measures of success. Similarly, the participants were then invited to look at the list of limitations or negative points raised on both poles of centralised and decentralised Human Resources departments. The task was to design action steps to eliminate or limit the impact of the negative aspects on each of the two poles. Since both poles were now included as being positive and useful, an important recognition was that there should be general agreement on the consequences of being overfocused on one pole to the detriment and neglect of the other. More detailed work would be needed to design measurable "early warning" indicators that cautioned against stepping into the downside of either pole (see Figure 9.2).

	Centralised pole	Decentralised pole
Positive aspects	**Action steps** to maximise the positive attributes of the centralised pole.	**Action steps** to maximise the positive attributes of the decentralised pole.
Negative aspects	**Early warnings** of undesirable consequences in the centralised pole, and **action steps** to limit/eliminate impact.	**Early warnings** of undesirable consequences in the decentralised pole, and **action steps** to limit/eliminate impact.

Figure 9.2 Use of a polarity map to clarify necessary actions. Source: Client data mapped according to the basic format used in Johnson (2014: 3–17).

Overall, the outcome of the workshop was an agreement to design a *"both-and"* solution using the data on their flipcharts as the foundation. While certain members of the workshop were still committed to their "either-or" position, they were overwhelmed by the decision of the majority in the room to work on the finer details of building a centralised HR management body located in head office, with decentralised bodies in the subsidiaries, and regulating the fields of operation and communication protocols between the two poles.

There are many such polarities to be found, best viewed not as problems to be solved, but as solutions – or polarities – to be managed. Take a look at the list of polarities below and consider your preferences for one or the other pole. Ask yourself: what are the advantages in each pole? What is the disadvantage in having too strong an emphasis on one pole to the detriment of the other?

Masculine vs feminine.
Logic vs intuition.
Detail vs big picture.
Directive vs consultative.
Stability vs change.
Cost savings vs product quality.
Individual decision making vs collective agreement.
Rational thinking vs feeling.
Firm vs flexible.
Differentiation vs integration.
Centralised vs decentralised.

Anyone who would welcome more insights into polarity work could not do better than reading Barry Johnson's 2014 book on polarity management, and his more recent 2020 publication, *And: Making a Difference by Leveraging Polarity, Paradox or Dilemma*. The latter work, in line with the best of Integral thinking, emphasises the importance to individuals, communities, and nations of recognising connection (the relationship of parts and wholes), and gives deeply moving examples of the healing value of *both-and* thinking.

Chapter 10 brings into focus all the steps of the dance in this Integral approach for transformative leadership.

Chapter 10

In conclusion

The value of the four-quadrant model

Integral vision is widely praised by the range of authors cited in this book for its emphasis on *inter-connection*, and its capacity to include every element and angle of human experience. The foundational element of the Integral Operating System – the quadrants – choreographs the steps of the dance in a turbulent environment: embracing subjective and inter-subjective experience, and their objective and inter-objective manifestations. The use of the quadrants is further enhanced by the deep insights for personal and professional development offered by the Enneagram. The purpose of this meta-model is to enlarge the experience of leaders at every level in an organisation in building a culture of adaptability and emotional resilience, a culture that embodies psychological safety.

There is constant flow among the quadrants – Wilber cautions that when one quadrant is unhealthy or out of balance, it affects the stability and wellbeing of all the other quadrants. For example, there currently exist groups who are environmentally conscious and deeply committed as *individuals* in their values (upper-left quadrant) and *behaviours* (upper-right quadrant) as well as *collectively* sharing commitment (lower-left quadrant) to changes that limit environmental damage. They recognise, with deep unhappiness and frustration, that our *systems and structures* may not yet be equal to the task of managing environmental damage (lower-right quadrant). As is already evident, the rising frustration in some of these groups and the strength of their shared values and commitment has resulted in their acting on the imbalance they perceive, attacking lower-right quadrant systems by disrupting transport, blocking roads, and throwing paint onto the premises of businesses they believe are complicit in environmental damage.

To lead, coach, consult, or facilitate in an organisation aspiring to inclusivity, high levels of engagement, and high performance means a commitment of leaders to cultivate their own development, and that of their staff – in a nutshell, the commitment and encouragement to build and practise self-awareness and a nuanced awareness of others (Petrie, 2020). A good starting point is to become familiar with the foundational element of Wilber's Integral Operating System, the four quadrants. Their significance and value in diagnosing, planning, and evaluating just

DOI: 10.4324/9781003377221-11

about any circumstance cannot be overestimated. They show the interconnections that are always present. As Wilber (2001c: 49) describes, "Individual conscious-ness is inextricably intermeshed with the objective organism and brain (upper-right quadrant); with nature, social systems and environment (lower-right quadrant); and with cultural settings, communal values, and worldviews (lower-left quadrant)." Making sure we consciously reflect in each quadrant space when diagnosing, planning, and evaluating ensures at the simplest level that we consider individual thoughts and feelings, individual behaviours, shared values and intentions, sys-tems, material context, and outcomes. We endeavour to make sure we have no blind spots in the consideration of a situation, or designing a plan, or evaluating outcomes.

Coaching on the quadrants

Chapter 1 starts with an example of a company whose managing director initiated a process of growing awareness, starting with himself. He believed there needed to be some sort of initiative, some sort of overhaul, to improve the overall per-formance of his company. He had started coaching for himself primarily as an opportunity to explore his thinking, and had come to a resolution over managing the discontent in the company. In his awareness at that time, there was a need to reframe the employees' disgruntled perception of the culture of the organisation – the question was how to go about doing this.

In the MD's first coaching sessions, he was introduced to Wilber's Integral quadrants – not as theory, but as a practical means to help him *diagnose* the circum-stances in the company. I drew the quadrants on the whiteboard in his boardroom, and then asked him some questions, indicating the appropriate quadrant as I asked each one:

Upper-left quadrant: What is a core value of yours in your role?
Upper-right quadrant: How does it show up in your management style, your leadership?
Lower-left quadrant: What are your shared values and intentions with your ExCo? What are your shared values and intentions with the employees?
Lower-right quadrant: How are these intentions showing up in your business outcomes?

He could answer the two first questions about himself easily, but then fell silent, looking perplexed at the last three. He quickly realised that he had made assump-tions that his ExCo saw matters the way he did, that he had hoped to find a top–down solution to the company's problems and that he had not considered the value of finding out from employees their perceptions of the workplace. He also realised that in his assessment of the business, and likely in that of his executive team, half of the quadrants were almost entirely absent in his awareness – the upper-left quad-rant of individual values, hopes, fears and ambitions, and the lower-left quadrant, the place of shared connection, shared intention, and shared values. When asked if he knew what his employees thought or felt or wanted, he looked startled and said, "I have no idea." What *he* wanted was better results for the business!

He shared his fresh insights gained from his introduction to the quadrants with his four ExCo colleagues, and suggested that all five of them experience coaching and, in particular, get to know the perspective from each quadrant and how to apply these to planning the proposed cultural transformation project. The overall value of coaching the ExCo team would be judged by the successful implementation of this project.

As described in Chapter 1, prior to his colleagues commencing their coaching journey, we agreed to meet to discuss the implementation of the transformation initiative, and each ExCo member's role in ensuring its success. In principle, everyone agreed that, if successful, the result would be company-wide buy-in to its core values, vision, and mission in order to achieve ambitious strategic objectives. No one could agree, however, on the reasons that this buy-in was currently missing, or what to do about it. Furthermore, as they argued and talked over one another, it was clear that no one was *listening* to one another.

Each contributed their ideas from a familiar and preferred perspective – in quadrant language, as the MD had become aware, the preferred perspective was an emphasis on the upper-right quadrant of actions and management behaviour, and the lower-right quadrant with its focus on systems, outputs, and production. Nobody listened, truly listened, beyond their own opinions. So, before the ExCo, as a team, could even begin to diagnose their current situation, they needed to adopt the discipline and practice of establishing a *listening culture*.

Chapter 6 describes the powerful thinking and productivity it is possible to achieve when a group of people are truly listening to one another, without interruption and with the commitment to share the airtime fairly. As mentioned, there are several exponents of creating a listening culture. The meta-model for transformative leadership advocated throughout this book, as stated in the Introduction, embraces Nancy Kline's principles and practices in creating a Thinking Environment®.

Once the conditions for listening to one another were established, each of the five ExCo members was asked to complete their own four-quadrant enquiry, which they then shared with one another – the kinds of question are described and set out in Chapter 1. Notable was the calm attention that had now replaced the earlier atmosphere of anxiety and competition. This initial introduction to working with the quadrants, with their demonstrable usefulness, provided the foundation for the coaching conversations with each ExCo member over the next six months.

The usefulness of knowing one's sweet spots and blind spots

Chapter 2 introduces Eric, Head of Operations, and the way in which coaching focused his awareness on his quadrant "sweet spots" and "blind spots". Beginning with the upper-left quadrant, he was invited to describe his qualities and values, an exercise which he found deeply uncomfortable. He was not used to thinking about himself in a reflective manner; even harder was having to articulate what he considered his positive qualities. He was much more comfortable describing his upper-right quadrant: what he did, his areas of expertise, how he showed up as a senior manager, what he considered his management style to be, and how he wanted to be seen in the business. His comments on the lower-left quadrant were mechanical and stunted, like quoting a company manual on values and intentions rather than being able to comment on what he truly felt was shared among his ExCo colleagues and with employees in general. He was also comfortable when talking about policy, practices, and systems (the lower-right quadrant), but was not as fluent as his account of his upper-right quadrant. Over time, with a growing awareness of his blind spots, he was able to reframe an adversarial relationship with a colleague sufficiently to see the value of their different approaches. He didn't realise just how accurate he was when he commented, "We just see the world a bit differently."

In Laura Divine's detailed description of the methodology of Integral Coaching Canada Inc. (Divine, 2009: 41–67), she points out that in Integrally informed coaching, the four-quadrant lenses are used in two ways: firstly, to understand the client's preference for particular quadrants, and how they interpret the other quadrants from this preferred perspective, and secondly, to assess the range or level of competency demonstrated by the client in each quadrant. Eric's preference for the upper-right quadrant space of action, of getting things done, showed up in his being reliable, accurate, and effective, as he expected himself to be. His colleague Anton's sweet spot was the lower-right quadrant, focusing on systems and understanding how things work together; and when new data came in that Anton considered important to integrate, it sometimes caused delays on previously agreed deadlines. This inevitably upset Eric and his sense of commitment; however, because Eric also valued the smooth running of systems and processes, he could now grudgingly appreciate Anton's perspective.

The shadow side of Eric's upper-right quadrant preference for action, for getting things done and done correctly, was that his management style was dogmatic, judgemental, and rigid. His mindset or level of vertical development fitted the description of Expert (described in Chapter 8, and renamed by Susanne Cook-Greuter as *skill-centric*), which was appropriate in his role. It was unlikely, and not strictly necessary as Head of Operations, that Eric would enlarge his outlook or change his values sufficiently to embrace the expanded mindset range of the Achiever – someone who takes pride in mastery, likes to be liked, and is usually a good team-player who enjoys achieving in collaboration with others. The focus of Eric's coaching was to soften the edges of his rigid ways of judging right and wrong, and to affirm what was effective and honourable in his behaviour, while encouraging him to *develop* his people more, rather than *telling* them exactly what to do. The leverage for influencing Eric in softening his hard edges lay in his desire to always do the right thing, and to have the approval of his peers and the MD. He was encouraged to find ways to *affirm* his staff in leading them to achieve the outcomes he expected, to replace harsh critical language with acknowledgement for what could genuinely be appreciated, before going on to reinforce the outcomes he expected.

Shifting levels

Melinda (the subject of Chapter 3), on the other hand, was able to show as an outcome of her coaching a shift from Expert as leader to embracing elements of the Achiever. One of her focus practices was to recognise and show compassion for the feelings of others, as well as for herself – to shift from a low range of emotional awareness with its focus on "me", "my needs", to a more inclusive capacity to hold others in her awareness with empathy. As with Eric, it was important for her, in her role as middle manager and team leader, to recognise that an increase in emotional intelligence did not mean a decrease in performance standards. Over time and with focused practice, she was able to reframe her interactions with a headstrong direct report from adversarial to willing engagement. She learned the value of giving appreciation, keeping it relevant, brief, and genuine – that it did not make her look "weak"; of asking the right questions to encourage her direct report to think, rather than angrily telling her; and of following up, if necessary, with a two-way conversation on what might still need to be achieved.

Mediating interpersonal conflict

A critical feature of Integral thought is the emphasis on *both-and* thinking, the ability to recognise one's opinions and beliefs as *true but partial*. Being willing to accept one's position or strong beliefs in this light mitigates the hostility that often arises in individuals and groups towards an adversarial stance. However, as can be seen in conflicts around the world, the ability to voluntarily entertain *both-and* thinking is not widely in evidence. It is therefore reasonable to expect that leaders at every level in an organisation may need some training in mediating conflict. As a mediator, it is a consciously acquired skill to overcome one's own temptation to bias and be willing to acknowledge the truthfulness felt by each person in conflict with another. Chapter 4 introduces a bitter conflict between a team member and a colleague. Working with the Integral quadrants, each person is evidently being truthful regarding the impact the conflict and its causes has on them (upper-left quadrant), and each person can cite evidence for their claims – the truth (upper-right quadrant). What neither could see was the picture from the other's point of view, in large part because each individually had made up her mind that what she saw was the whole story – so what would be the point of asking the other for their perspective? Each person, separately, was asked to populate the four quadrants with their version of events, and permission was sought from each to share this picture with their adversary. The separate sessions with each person involved gave an opportunity for the intensity of their emotions to subside over time, once each had been respectfully heard. The ground was laid for proposing a mediation session, after each had seen the other's four-quadrant mapping of their version of events. This did not yet reconcile them to each other. That came only after their acceptance that in their versions of events, as they had truthfully experienced them, each had not been aware of a critical piece missing from their own view but present in the other's perspective. Their view in each case had been *true – but partial*.

Creating the terms for inclusivity

Chapter 5 describes the steps a company took to dismantle a climate of distrust and demotivation and co-create a culture of inclusion. The workshop process disclosed the impact of an entrenched ideology of superiority in one group on the self-esteem and wellbeing of those not included as members of that group. The pattern of top–down communications was redesigned to include a two-way bottom–up/top–down stream. Two key issues that had negatively impacted the establishment of a healthy organisational culture, perceptions of race and gender, were openly addressed, with religion and culture playing their parts as well. The overwhelming consensus was to agree on a baseline value asserting the right of each person, regardless of identity, to equality of respect.

Two years later, there was an outburst where racist cultural perceptions emerged again. What went wrong? The head of Risk Management had taken on a new hire, a personal assistant whose legal knowledge and level of efficiency had been highly recommended. At a high-level meeting to discuss avoiding financial risk in a potentially ill-advised investment, the head of Risk Management was seeking to trace the source of flawed or incomplete research on the suspect investment. The new personal assistant named someone responsible for the potential financial risk, stating in a heated manner that the person in question was typical of that race: devious, unreliable, open to bribery, and never to be trusted. After the outburst, there was an uncomfortable silence.

One of the senior participants at the meeting was a member of the slandered racial group, a highly regarded employee of some years' standing in the organisation. In his own account of the event, he was stunned by the vitriol in the outburst, but what hurt him the most was that no one at that meeting, including the head of Risk Management with whom he had worked closely over the years, criticised the racial outburst at the time. The body language of some even seemed to be signalling satisfaction. The aggrieved member took his version of the incident to the head of Human Resources and asked for an intervention – at the very least, a process that addressed the negative stereotyping by the offending individual, and reminded everyone at that meeting of the extensive workshop processes over the previous two years and achievements in working towards a company culture free of racial and gender stereotypes.

An important recognition was that there was *no induction process* at the intake of new hires that addressed the prevalence of racial or gender bias in society at large. Furthermore, new hires were not made aware, as a matter of company policy, of the agreements reached at the workshops that had cascaded throughout the organisation during the previous two years. When called into a meeting with a senior member of Human Resources, the offender was unrepentant, claiming that several others in the company agreed with his assessment of "those people". The fact that equality of respect for each employee's identity was clearly printed as one of the core company values was as meaningless as a health warning on a smoker's packet of cigarettes.

It was a disturbing reminder that we can change the rulebook, but that is not sufficient to change hearts and minds. When the injured party was asked the reason he did not speak up (not just for himself but on behalf of his fellow employees), he said that in spite of himself, he felt silenced by the fact that the head of Risk Management, a white man, had said nothing to rebuke his new hire, also white. In his view, the ideology of superiority had been implicitly reinstated, triggering an instant recall of decades of being treated as inferior.

A proposal was made for a facilitated session to be held with all the participants of that Risk Management meeting, to revisit the pernicious effect of an ideology of superiority based on an arbitrary indicator like skin colour (a lower-left quadrant exercise to affirm connections, shared values, and intentions). It was also agreed that the offending new hire be offered coaching, where he might find parallels in his own life where someone or some group had had the power to reduce his self-esteem and reflect on what that had felt like (an upper-left quadrant process of creating self-awareness), hopefully leading the individual to a commitment to practise new behaviours (upper-right quadrant). Last, but by no means least, was the undertaking to restructure induction (paying attention to the systemic lower-right quadrant) to include a commitment by all new hires to live the company values.

The incident was an important reminder to revisit the lived meaning of company values with employees, not just when there was a crisis, but as an opportunity for staff to share experiences and perceptions on a regular basis. Coming together would also serve to remind them of the relational qualities that are so important to each person in realising their potential. What affects potential? The neuroscientist, Professor Paul Brown, has a resounding answer: "Quality and consistency of relationship ... the brain is the organ of relationship ... all effective leadership is about relationship" (Brown and Hales, 2011: 39).

Psychological safety and building a listening culture

Creating psychological safety in organisations and in teams includes the opportunity for individuals to recover from the negative impact of limiting assumptions about themselves and others. It was fortunate in the example of racial abuse above that there was a willingness, a commitment, in Human Resources, to find ways to uphold the agreements that had felt so positive for the company when they were made at those earlier workshops in search of a transformed organisation where psychological safety would be the ultimate lived value.

Just as important at induction of new hires as being made aware of company values is the ongoing *practising* of a listening culture. As described in Chapter 6, the benefit of creating a listening culture is to raise the emotional intelligence of every employee at every level, simply by pre-empting disruptive and poorly thought-through interjections. An executive in the fishing industry, responsible for health and safety, decided to implement the conditions for a listening culture with teams in his work environment. His first experiment at work was a meeting with his direct reports. He had prepared the agenda in the form of questions, having realised for himself the difference in brain engagement when in the presence of a question, rather than a bland header like "Customer Service" or "Financials".

Before displaying the agenda or explaining in any detail the rules of engagement, he launched into actively demonstrating. He told his team of eight that he wanted to hear from each of them in a round, starting on his left, anything that they were pleased with since their last weekly meeting. He emphasised that he wanted to hear only what was positive for each of them in this round, asked that no one interrupt, and that each person limit their contribution to a headline. They responded well, except when one or two members had wanted to launch into what was not going so well for them. He reassured them that their concerns would be heard – in good time. At the completion of that round, he told the group of his experience of being listened to without interruption, of being asked key questions at the appropriate moments that took his thinking to a new level and enabled him to come up with solutions to problems he had been going over and over in his head. The group agreed to commit to not interrupting one another, also not repeating one another, and to sharing airtime evenly. The noticeable outcome from this first experiment with his team was the improved quality of thinking in their contributions; the simple fact that no one was interrupted, and everyone was encouraged to participate equally, seemed to raise the quality of the team's contributions to the agenda questions.

His next challenge was to implement this way of meeting with the employees on the factory floor: some illiterate, many wary of authority figures, all used to being instructed and told what was expected of them. He was surprised to find an even better response than with his direct reports. There was almost overwhelming appreciation of being asked what each person thought, and then having equality of time to contribute to health and safety issues, especially emerging from COVID-19 conditions. In his words:

> It proved to be a perfect time, and provided an antidote to the varying challenges I've faced in my personal and professional lives. Thanks to the sessions, I've really felt empowered, and my working practice and mindset have changed for the better. Tips on how to hold meetings more effectively were immediately popular with my team. It's not just the participation that has increased, but also the quality and enthusiasm of the engagements.

The Enneagram, introduced in Chapter 7, offers an engaging way of enhancing self-awareness and increasing relationship intelligence. The individual profiles give highlights of positive characteristics, as well as pointing out developmental areas and offering advice on practices to be more mindful of self and others. In a team context, sharing Enneagram profiles is a great way to raise relational skills among team members as people gain more insight into one another.

In considering leadership consciousness, leaders and coaches are increasingly aware of taking into account stages of adult development, the topic of Chapter 8. A key marker of accelerated consciousness development is the ability to hold multiple perspectives, to be open to ideas that differ wildly from one's own, and to manage one's emotions. It does not follow, however, that a senior manager or technically brilliant team leader will be capable of greater emotional maturity than a younger, less experienced staff member. The theories and wisdoms of researchers into stages of adult development discussed in Chapter 8 are readily available; however, these can be complex to assimilate, and it can be difficult to know how to translate descriptors of stages of adult development into simple everyday life, to convert theory into accessible practice. Works such as *Changing on the Job: Developing Leaders for a Complex World* (Garvey Berger, 2012) and *Developmental Coaching: Working with the Self* (Bachkirova, 2011) have done just this – they offer practical guidelines on how to recognise and work with simplified key levels of development. Other great resources are to be found online, including papers and articles by Barrett C. Brown (2005, 2013) and Nick Petrie (2013, 2020), and the website of the Centre for Creative Leadership.

Polarity management, explored in Chapter 9, is a powerful solution to the challenge of managing conflict, especially over what appears to be an insoluble problem. The gift of Barry Johnson's (2014) polarity management approach is its ability to include multiple mindsets in resolving conflicts and arriving at mutually acceptable outcomes.

What is a "teal" organisation?

The "momentous leap" in consciousness predicted by Clare Graves (1974) is a major shift "above the dotted line" into second-tier levels of consciousness (discussed in Chapter 8). The first of these is named by Wilber as "teal" consciousness. Looking through an organisational lens, Frédéric Laloux (2014) describes how a "teal" organisation differs from conventional corporate structures. At this level of organisation, while there is still a hierarchy, there are no rigid reporting lines between teams and managers. Decision making is distributed throughout the organisation, with the caveat that decision-makers at all levels seek input from experts and from all those affected by their decision making before implementation. Roles are flexible, defined by a common purpose.

At the systemic level, considerable work is required in gradual stages over time. However, process and design changes are not sufficient in themselves to create a "teal" organisation. "Teal" is not simply a cognitive concept. Without the personal mindset at top leadership level that truly *embodies* teal principles as *lived practices*, the aspiration of achieving a genuinely "teal" organisation is unlikely to be met.

An example of the challenges in aiming for a "teal" company culture

A key area of focus for the MD of a digital design company was to develop her leaders at several levels to have strong coaching competencies. In her vision for her company, part of an international organisation and consisting of several teams and their leaders, she aimed to build capacity in the senior and middle levels of leadership to have decision making distributed throughout the company. To her surprise, far from welcoming her planned changes in the culture of the company, her top leaders found their more distributed role to be more taxing, certainly at first, than in a traditional organisational hierarchy.

One of the functions of the executive was to ensure that all teams and their members had a mutually nominated team leader for every project – and, depending on the particular skills required, this team leadership role may have been only for the duration of a particular project before the mantle was passed on to the next most appropriate person to head up a specific project. This "revolving leadership" plan caused considerable unhappiness, to the extent that some of the established team leaders were considering their career choices, and whether it might be time to find a different company. In a meeting with some of those who would be affected by the proposed changes, they talked of feeling downgraded, insecure, even betrayed by a leadership they had thought they were supporting up to the hilt.

There was ongoing training with team leaders to help them reframe their roles more positively, initially by creating a listening culture. They built their capacity as the role-players who enabled members in their teams to communicate more effectively with one another. By adopting the conditions of a listening culture, each team member was given time to learn how to participate in distributed decision making. The senior leader's role in the decision-making process was anything but hands-off or "downgraded", as some ExCo members and team leaders in the company had feared. Far from becoming redundant – a fear which negatively affected their ability to delegate, and also their willingness to nurture growth – their leadership responsibility was a four-quadrant requirement: to grow the wisdom and self-control to foster sound decision-making practices among their team leaders, and to ensure that team members also acquired requisite skills.

Team leaders were encouraged to source appropriate skills needed for a particular project either internally, or externally, depending on budgets. They encouraged team members to be knowledgeable about the state of the budget and spending limits, and to consider others beyond their team who may have been affected by decisions taken. Having teams take responsibility for understanding contractual obligations, and managing budgets and financial planning wisely, was a learning curve for all team leaders and their teams – especially as team leadership was changeable depending on the project skills needed. Senior leaders were also expected to support teams by providing or helping source information about clients and stakeholders.

The frustrations were many – for example, a client enlarged the parameters of a project design but resisted increasing the contract budget, putting strain on the timelines for deliverables and the ability of the team to deliver quality work within deadlines. Ultimately, in line with the best of coaching, the executive leader's role was to ask the good, open questions that encouraged team leaders and their people to think well for themselves – and these senior leaders were having to learn to be prepared to live with team decisions that they perhaps would not have made themselves, but which they recognised would not sink the ship.

While initially there was immense enthusiasm within the executive aligned around a common purpose, the most challenging part of this transformational journey was the first few months, indeed most of the first year, under the new MD. Under stress, managers tended to default to more familiar directive behaviours that may have been destructive to emergent trust in the new "rules of the game". The first step of the journey was a commitment to make opportunities to keep practising behaviours and attitudes that enabled senior leaders and team leaders to hear one another differently and listen deeply without letting premature judgment get in the way. It was a practice that, over time, steadily raised emotional intelligence by placing a mindfulness buffer between ill-considered reactions or impulsive interruptions, and a thoughtful response.

People at every level were invited to populate their four-quadrant template with their thinking. Through new openness to one another's views, a more comprehensive diagnosis of a current situation was possible, one that included the four perspectives of the Integral quadrants: individual values, beliefs, and feelings; individual behaviours and skills in use, and management style; shared intentions and values; and the systems and the outputs. One-on-one coaching also helped each person translate their quadrant insights into actions. Group sessions then consolidated the outcomes with measures designed and commitments made to carry them out.

Mending broken connections

The personalities and case studies in this book describe typical representations of dysfunction in organisational culture: on the whole, low-trust environments with a consequent impact on performance. The pattern is that of connections broken by executive teams in the development of their managers, and by managers in the support and development of their staff. There appears to be an overwhelming emphasis on outputs (lower-right quadrant), with rather less attention to the congruence of outputs with the espoused organisational culture (lower-left quadrant), and little attention to congruence between individual beliefs (upper-left quadrant) and manifest behaviours (upper-right quadrant).

In working with leaders at different levels and in different organisations, the case studies in this book have described a process of initially surfacing issues through individual coaching sessions, and then sharing the same with appropriate teams or groups. The interventions aim first and foremost at transforming a particular range of leadership competencies – *relational intelligence*. The intervention for leader-as-coach comprises several interlocking steps drawing on Wilber's Integral vision, which have been described in each of the book's chapters. Wilber asserts that in leadership, in the world, the leading edge *is* Integral because it transcends and includes all the other stages of human development, and is the only framework that truly understands and works for human connection – unity in diversity. Best of all, with awareness and a commitment to self-development, it is within the capacity of leaders at the top to harness the positive qualities of leadership needed at every level in an organisation, releasing the potential in every mindset, at every stage of development.

Bibliography

Aiken, D.E. (2009). *Towards coaching across divides to create alliances: An integral approach.* Unpublished Doctorate in Professional Studies dissertation. London: Institute of Work-Based Learning, University of Middlesex.

Allas, T., and Schaninger, B. (2020). The boss factor: Making the world a better place through workplace relationships. *McKinsey Quarterly*, 22 September. URL: https://www.mckinsey.com/capabilities/people-and-organizational-performance/our-insights/the-boss-factor-making-the-world-a-better-place-through-workplace-relationships.

Almaas, A.H. (2021). *Keys to the Enneagram: How to unlock the highest potential of every personality type.* Boulder, CO: Shambhala.

Alston, E., Alston, L.J., and Mueller, B. (2020). Leadership within organisational hierarchies. *SSRN Electronic Journal*, July, 1–46. DOI: 10.2139/ssrn.3549964.

Anderson, R.J., and Adams, W.A. (2019). *Scaling leadership: Building organisational capability and capacity to create outcomes that matter most.* Hoboken, NJ: Wiley.

Angier, M., and Axelrod, B. (2014). Realising the power of talented women. *McKinsey Quarterly*, 1 September. URL: www.mckinsey.com/capabilities/people-and-organizational-performance/our-insights/realizing-the-power-of-talented-women.

Anthony, E.L. (2017). The impact of leadership coaching on leadership behaviours. *Journal of Management Development*, 36(7):930–939. DOI: 10.1108/JMD-06-2016-0092.

Ashkenas, R. (2013). Change management needs to change. *Harvard Business Review*, 16 April, 2013(3): 20–23.

Bachkirova, T. (2011). *Developmental coaching: Working with the self.* Maidenhead: Open University Press.

Bass, B.M., and Avolio, B.J. (1994). *Improving organisational effectiveness through transformational leadership.* Thousand Oaks, CA: SAGE.

Beck, D.E., and Cowan, C.C. (2000). *Spiral dynamics: Mastering values, leadership, and change.* Oxford: Blackwell.

Beckes, L., Coan, J.A., and Hasselmo, K. (2013). Familiarity promotes the blurring of self and other in the neural representation of threat. *Social Cognitive and Affective Neuroscience*, 8(6):670–677. DOI: 10.1093/scan/nss046.

Bennett, K. (2017). *Living and leading through uncertainty: Developing leaders' capability for uncertainty.* Randburg: Knowres.

Bennis, W. (2007). The challenges of leadership in the modern world: Introduction to the special issue. *American Psychologist*, 62(1):2–5.

Blake, A. (2018). *Your body is your brain: Leverage your somatic intelligence to find purpose, build resilience, deepen relationships and lead more powerfully*. Kindle edition. Truckee, CA: Trokay Press.

Boeree, C.G. (2009). General psychology: Moral development: Kohlberg's theory. *The basics of psychology: An online primer*. Shippensburg, PA: Psychology Department, Shippensburg University. URL: webspace.ship.edu/cgboer/genpsymoraldev.html.

Brown, B.C. (2005). Theory and practice of integral sustainable development: Values, developmental levels, and natural design. *Journal of Integral Theory and Practice*, 1(2):1–70.

Brown, B.C. (2013). *The future of leadership for conscious capitalism*. Sebastopol, CA: MetaIntegral Associates.

Brown, P., and Hales, B. (2011). Neuroscience: New science for new leadership. *Developing Leaders*, 5:36–42.

Butcher, J. (2012). Exploring the link between identity and coaching practice. *International Journal of Evidence-Based Coaching and Mentoring*, Special Issue No. 6, 119–129.

Cavanagh, M.J., and Lane, D.A. (2012). Coaching psychology coming of age: The challenges we face in the messy world of complexity. *International Coaching Psychology Review*, 7(1):75–90.

Chapman, L. (2010). *Integrated experiential coaching: Becoming an executive coach*. London: Karnac.

Cook-Greuter, S.R. (1994). Rare forms of self-understanding in mature adults. In Miller, M.E., and Cook-Greuter, S.R. (eds.), *Transcendence and mature thought in adulthood: The further reaches of adult development* (pp. 119–146). Lanham, MD: Rowman and Littlefield.

Cook-Greuter, S.R. (2004). Making the case for a developmental perspective. *Industrial and Commercial Training*, 36(7):275–281. DOI: 10.1108/00197850410563902.

Cook-Greuter, S.R. (2005). *Ego development: Nine levels of increasing embrace*. Unpublished monograph. Wayland, MA: II Psychology Centre.

Cook-Greuter, S.R. (2018). The construct-aware stage of ego development and its relationship to the fool archetype. *Integral Review*, 14(1):300–310.

DeVos, C.W. (2020). Looking back: The best of 2020. *IntegralLife.com*. URL: integrallife.com/looking-back-the-best-of-2020/.

Divine, L. (2009). Looking at and looking as the client: The quadrants as a type structure lens. *Journal of Integral Theory and Practice*, 4(1):21–40.

Duhigg, C. (2016). What Google learned from its quest to build the perfect team. *New York Times Magazine*, The Work Issue, 25 February. URL: www.nytimes.com/2016/02/28/magazine/what-google-learned-from-its-quest-to-build-the-perfect-team.html.

Enders, G. (2015). *Gut: The inside story of our body's most under-rated organ*. Translated by David Shaw. London: Scribe.

Edmondson, A.C. (2019). *The fearless organisation: Creating psychological safety in the workplace for earning, innovation, and growth*. Kindle edition. Hoboken, NJ: Wiley.

Edwards, M. (2003). *A brief history of holons*. URL: www.integralworld.net/edwards13.html.

Edwards, M. (2009). *Organisational transformation for sustainability: An integral metatheory*. New York: Routledge.

Endrejat, P.C., and Burnes, B. (2022). Draw it, check it, change it: Reviving Lewin's topology to facilitate organisational change theory and practice. *Journal of Applied Behavioural Science*, August, 1–26. DOI: 10.1177/00218863221122875.

Feldman Barrett, L. (2017). *How emotions are made: The secret life of the brain*. Kindle edition. London: Macmillan.

Feldman Barrett, L. (2020). *Seven-and-a-half lessons about the brain*. New York: Houghton Mifflin Harcourt.

Frost, L. (2009). Integral perspectives on coaching: An analysis of integral coaching Canada across eight zones and five methodologies. *Journal of Integral Theory and Practice*, 4(1):93–120.

Garvey Berger, J. (2012). *Changing on the job: Developing leaders for a complex world*. Kindle edition. Stanford, CA: Stanford University Press.

Garvey Berger, J. (2019). *Unlocking leadership mindtraps: How to thrive in complexity*. Stanford, CA: Stanford University Press.

Glaser, J.E. (2014). *Conversational intelligence: How great leaders build trust and get extraordinary results*. Abingdon, Oxon: Bibliomotion.

Goleman, D. (1996). *Emotional intelligence: Why it can matter more than IQ*. London: Bloomsbury.

Goleman, D. (2000). Leadership that gets results. *Harvard Business Review*, March–April, 78(2):78–90.

Goleman, D., and Boyatzis, R. (2017). Emotional intelligence has 12 elements - Which do you need to work on? *Harvard Business Review*, 84(2):1–5.

Goleman, D., Boyatzis, R., and McKee, A. (2002). *The new leaders: Transforming the art of leadership into the science of results*. Boston, MA: Little, Brown.

Goleman, D., Boyatzis, R., and McKee, A. (2013). *Primal leadership: Unleashing the power of emotional intelligence*. Tenth anniversary edition. Boston, MA: Harvard Business School Publishing.

Graves, C. (1974). Human nature prepares for a momentous leap. *Futurist*, April, 8(2):72–87.

Hawkins, P., and Smith, N. (2013). *Coaching, mentoring and organisational consultancy: Supervision, skills and development*. Second edition. Maidenhead: Open University Press.

Hildebrandt, T.H., Campone, F., Norwood, K., and Ostrowski, E.J. (eds.) (2020). *Innovations in leadership coaching: Research and practice*. Santa Barbara, CA: Fielding University Press.

Hunt, J. (2009). Transcending and including our current way of being: An introduction to integral coaching. *AQAL Journal*, 4(1):1–20.

Ibarra, H., and Scoular, A. (2019). The leader as coach. *Harvard Business Review*, 97(6):110–119.

Israel, T. (2020). How to listen – Really listen – To someone you don't agree with. *ideas.ted .com*, 12 October. URL: ideas.ted.com/how-to-listen-really-listen-to-someone-you-dont -agree-with/.

Jaques, E., and Clement, S.D. (1997). *Executive leadership: A practical guide to managing complexity*. Arlington, VA: Carson Hall.

Jeremiah, D. (2016). Mindful meetings: How to bring your best leadership brain to work. *GE.com*, 11 October. URL: www.ge.com/news/reports/mindful-meetings-how-to-bring -your-best-leadership-brain-to-work.

Johnson, B. (2014). *Polarity management: Identifying and managing unsolvable problems*. Amherst, MA: HRD Press.

Johnson, B. (2020). *And: Making a difference by leveraging polarity, paradox or dilemma: Volume one: Foundations*. Amherst, MA: HRD Press.

Jones, H.E., Chesley, J.A., and Egan, T. (2020). Helping leaders grow up: Vertical leadership development in practice. *Journal of Values-Based Leadership*, 13(1), Article 8. DOI: 10.22543/0733.131.1275.

Kahane, A.M. (2017). *Collaborating with the enemy: How to work with people you don't agree with or like or trust*. Oakland, CA: Berrett-Koehler.

Kegan, R. (1994). *In over our heads: The mental demands of modern life*. Cambridge, MA: Harvard University Press.

Kegan, R., and Lahey, L.L. (2001). *How the way we talk can change the way we work: Seven languages for transformation*. Kindle edition. San Francisco, CA: Jossey-Bass.

Kegan, R., and Lahey, L.L. (2016). *An everyone culture: Becoming a deliberately developmental organisation*. Boston, MA: Harvard Business Review Press.

Kline, N. (1999). *Time to think: Listening to ignite the human mind*. London: Cassell Hachette.

Kline, N. (2005). *Notes compiled by Dorrian Aiken from Time to Think training course*. Cape Town.

Kline, N. (2009). *More time to think: A way of being in the world*. Pool-in-Wharfedale: Fisher King.

Kline, N. (2020). *The promise that changes everything: I will not interrupt you*. London: Penguin Life.

Kline, N. (2022). *Personal email from Nancy Kline to Dorrian Aiken*, 18 February.

Kotter, J.P. (2012). *Leading change*. Boston, MA: Harvard Business Review Press.

Kupers, W., and Weibler, J. (2008). Emotions in organisation: An integral perspective. *International Journal of Work Organisation and Emotion*, 2(3):256–287.

Laloux, F. (2014). *Reinventing organisations: A guide to creating organisations inspired by the next stage of human consciousness*. Brussels: Nelson Parker.

Landrum, N.E., and Gardner, C.L. (2005). Using integral theory to effect strategic change. *Journal of Organisational Change Management*, 18(3):247–258. DOI: 10.1108/09534810510599407.

Landrum, N.E., and Gardner, C.L. (2012). An integral theory perspective on the firm. *International Journal of Business Insights and Transformation*, 4(3):74–79.

Lewin, K. (1943). Psychology and the process of group living. *The Journal of Social Psychology*, 17(1):113–131. DOI: 10.1080/00224545.1943.9712269.

Lewis, T., Amini, F., and Lannon, R. (2001). *A general theory of love*. New York: Vintage.

Lieberman, M.D., Rock, D., Grant Halvorson, H., and Cox, C. (2015). Breaking bias updated: The Seeds Model™. *NeuroLeadership Journal*, 6:1–18.

Lipton, B.H. (2015). *The biology of belief: Unleashing the power of consciousness, matter and miracles*. Tenth anniversary edition. New York: Hay House.

Maslow, A.H. (2011). *Hierarchy of needs: A theory of human motivation*. Kindle edition. www.all-about-psychology.com.

McGilchrist, I. (2010). *The master and his emissary: The divided brain and the making of the Western world*. Kindle edition. New Haven, CT: Yale University Press.

McLean, P. (2019). *Self as coach, self as leader: Developing the best in you to develop the best in others*. Hoboken, NJ: Wiley.

Morgan, J. (2015). The 5 types of organisational structures: Part 3, flat organisations. *Forbes .com*, 13 July. URL: www.forbes.com/sites/jacobmorgan/2015/07/13/the-5-types-of -organizational-structures-part-3-flat-organizations/?sh=206c73426caa.

NeuroLeadership Institute. (2022). 5 ways to spark (or destroy) your employees' motivation. *Your Brain At Work, Culture and Leadership*, 15 September. URL: neuroleadership .com/your-brain-at-work/scarf-model-motivate-your-employees.

Oshry, B. (2007). *Seeing systems: Unlocking the mysteries of organisational life*. Second edition. San Francisco, CA: Berrett-Koehler.

Patterson, K., Grenny, J., McMillan, R., and Switzler, A. (2002). *Crucial conversations: Tools for talking when the stakes are high.* New York: McGraw-Hill.

Petrie, N. (2013). *Vertical leadership development: Part 1: Developing leaders for a complex world.* White paper. Colorado Springs, CO: Centre for Creative Leadership.

Petrie, N. (2020). *Lessons in vertical leadership development.* White paper. Austin, TX: Nicholas Petrie, LLC. URL: www.nicholaspetrie.com/post/lessons-in-vertical-leadership -development.

Phelps, E.A., and Thomas, L.A. (2003). Race, behaviour, and the brain: The role of neuroimaging in understanding complex social behaviours. *Political Psychology,* 24(4):747–758. DOI: 10.1046/j.1467-9221.2003.00350.x.

Rhodes, S. (2006). *The Enneagram and Ken Wilber's integral kosmology.* Draft 13, 24 October. Unpublished paper. URL: kupdf.net/download/the-enneagram-and-ken -wilber-39-s-integral-kosmology_5b08d0f6e2b6f56966cd3afa_pdf.

Rhodes, S. (2013). *The integral Enneagram: A dharma-based approach for linking the nine personality types, nine stages of transformation and Ken Wilber's integral operating system.* Seattle, WA: Geranium Press.

Robertson, B.J. (2015). *Holacracy: The revolutionary management system that abolishes hierarchy.* London: Penguin.

Rock, D. (2008). SCARF®: A brain-based model for collaborating with and influencing others. *Neuroleadership Journal,* 1:1–9.

Rock, D. (2009). *Your brain at work: Strategies for overcoming distraction, regaining focus, and working smarter all day long.* New York: Harper Business.

Rock, D., and Cox, C. (2012). SCARF® in 2012: Updating the social neuroscience of collaborating with others. *NeuroLeadership Journal,* 4:1–14.

Rock, D., and Schwartz, J.M. (2006). A brain-based approach to coaching. *International Journal of Coaching in Organisations,* 4(2):32–43.

Rooke, D., and Torbert, W.R. (2005). Seven transformations of leadership. *Harvard Business Review,* April, 83(4): 67–76.

Sapolsky, R.M. (2017). *Behave: The biology of humans at our best and worst.* New York: Penguin.

Sharer, K. (2012). Why I'm a listener: Amgen CEO Kevin Sharer. *McKinsey Quarterly,* 1 April. URL: www.mckinsey.com/featured-insights/leadership/why-im-a-listener -amgen-ceo-kevin-sharer.

Siegel, D.J. (2017). *Mind: A journey to the heart of being human.* New York: Norton.

Siegel, D.J. (2018). *Aware: The science and practice of presence – The groundbreaking meditation practice.* New York: Tarcher Perigree.

Simcox, J. (2005). *Detailed descriptions of the developmental stages or action logics of the leadership development framework.* Presented at the W. Edwards Deming Research Institute, Eleventh Annual Research Seminar. New York: Graduate Business School, Fordham University.

Smuts, J.C. (2013). *Holism and evolution.* Reproduction of first edition. Gouldsboro, ME: Gestalt Journal Press.

Spayd, M.K., and Madore, M. (2021). *Agile transformation: Using the integral agile transformation framework™ to think and lead differently.* Boston, MA: Addison-Wesley.

Steyn, M.E. (2001). *"Whiteness just isn't what it used to be": White identity in a changing South Africa.* New York: State University of New York Press.

Torbert, W.R. (2004). *Action inquiry: The secret of timely and transforming leadership.* San Francisco, CA: Berrett-Koehler.

Wagner, J.P. (1996). *The Enneagram spectrum of personality styles: An introductory guide.* Portland, OR: Metamorphous Press.

Wagner, J.P. (2010). *Nine lenses on the world: The Enneagram perspective.* Evanston, IL: NineLens Press.

Waugh, R. (2012). Racism is "hardwired" into the human brain – And people can be prejudiced without knowing it. *Daily Mail,* Science, 26 June. URL: www.dailymail .co.uk/sciencetech/article-2164844/Racism-hardwired-human-brain--people-racists -knowing-it.html.

Whitmore, J. (2009). *Coaching for performance: GROWing human potential and purpose.* Fourth edition. London: Nicholas Brealey.

Wilber, K. (1998). *The marriage of sense and soul: Integrating science and religion.* New York: Random House.

Wilber, K. (2000). *Integral psychology: Consciousness, spirit, psychology and therapy.* Boston, MA: Shambhala.

Wilber, K. (2001a). *A brief history of everything.* Second edition. Dublin: Gateway.

Wilber, K. (2001b). *The eye of the spirit: An integral vision for a world gone slightly mad.* Third edition. Boston, MA: Shambhala.

Wilber, K. (2001c). *A theory of everything: An integral vision for business, politics, science and spirituality.* Boston, MA: Shambhala.

Wilber, K. (2015). The Darth Vader move. *Integral life,* Conversations podcast, 18 December. URL: integrallife.com/darth-vader-move/.

Index

Printed in the United States
by Baker & Taylor Publisher Services